Undefiled Intimacy

Christianity *Between* the Sheets

A candid discourse about the sensual side of the saint

By Chaz Kono

The rebirth of the bedroom *for the born-again believer.*

"<u>Marriage</u> is honorable among all and the <u>marriage bed</u> <u>UNDEFILED</u>; *but* fornicators and adulterers <u>GOD</u> WILL JUDGE".

<u>Hebrews 13:4</u>

Table of contents

—ᄴ—

Acknowledgements

—ᴍᴍ—

I'd simply like to thank my loving wife for her continuous encouragement and unselfish support. You still rock baby! I'd also like to send my love and gratitude to my family and friends in Brooklyn NY, Jersey City NJ, Atlanta GA, Fredericksburg & Richmond VA, Orlando FL and San Diego CA. To my small group family in Nor Cal thank you all for the support and prayer coverage. I love every one of you so dearly.

Dedication

—ɯɯ—

This book is dedicated to every Christian couple (husband & wife) who takes a hold of these pages and runs with it.

A woman's confession

—ᵐ—

Excerpt Interview with Lydia (Not her real name):

"There are periods of time where I feel like I can't do this anymore, but literally, I have stayed with my husband because of my kids. . . . I just really feel like it would just mess up their world too much. . . If I could leave, I would leave. In fact, I think if things were a perfect situation for me now, I would still leave. So, I guess, yes, on the one hand, I stay together because of the kids, but also because, what am I going to do alone with three kids? And where am I going to go and how am I going to support them? . . . I feel like I'm trapped a lot. We are a Christian couple and isn't that what Christians supposed to do, just grin and bear it till Jesus comes? So, I just put on a happy face and keep going. But not because I want to but because I feel like I'm forced, I feel like I have to, that I have no other options, at least no options that appeal to me in any way. . . . Are you going to trade a marriage that you're not happy in for a really hard life of being a single mom? . . . Can I just accept the way things are? It's not like I get beat up. It's not like I'm being abused in any way, other than I just feel like I have a loveless marriage, intimacy is nonexistent and although I'm not alone I feel extremely lonely. It's sad but I feel that we are just business partners; I can't remember the last time we had sex, kissed or even held hands—intimacy has vanished like a feather in the wind. He does his thing; I do my thing to help things move along for the family. Can I accept that? I still don't know if I can accept it. . ."

Disclaimer

—⟋⟍—

First and foremost I am a born again believer, redeemed by the shed blood of my Lord and Savior Jesus Christ. I am a Christian saved by God's amazing grace. I am also a twice divorced father of two; and I have also indulged my flesh in adultery and fornication. Although God has forgiven me I still cannot forget that I've failed miserably in the most sacred of unions. No one in their right mind decides to marry with high expectations of it failing or ending in divorce. The intent is stay married and to ride the waves of nirvana for as long as possible. I deeply regret the errors of my past yet in spite of my failures Gods word remains true. I firmly believe the Holy Bible is the irrefutable word of Almighty God given to mankind for the purposes set forth in II Timothy 3:16:

". . .profitable for doctrine, for reproof, for ***correction, and for instruction*** in righteousness that the man (and woman) of God may be COMPLETE, thoroughly equipped for every good work. . ."

The Holy Scriptures clearly delineate and acknowledge sexual intimacy between a **male** and a **female** married to one another in the Lord. Although many would disagree with the biblical interpretation or decree of marriage, any and all sexual relationships outside of this unambiguously defined biblical context is for God our creator to judge.

Premise

—ᗰᗰ—

Sex is one of the most prevalent and recurring themes in the Bible. The commentary you are about to be exposed to is not for the thin skinned or easily offended, although perhaps some will indeed be offended, it is for the most part straightforward and to the point. These are my humble and forthright opinions and suggestions and I suspect that some readers may find my presentation of these issues insufficiently balanced, inappropriate or even vulgar. You have the right to your opinion and I welcome your scrutiny. But as the old saying goes 'if the shoe fits wear it', only you and your significant other knows the 'ugly truth' about the level of intimacy in your home. Obviously, not all couples are alike but I believe we are similar enough to share or express most of what you will find on the pages to follow. Our commonalities outweigh our differences and this is the context in which I am writing. To wit, it is my hope that the 21st century church will go beyond its four walls and realize the need for frank discussions, which will translate into action, on this subject matter for the intimate healing, pleasure, and purpose of our marital unions

Far too many of our brothers and sisters, including myself, have fallen prey to the lures of lust, pornography, adultery and sex as the world and society defines or describes it. I believe we (the church) have a sensual side as well, one that is attractive, gratifying, erotic, stimulating, creative and most exciting of all undefiled. We (the church of the living God) should be the standard bearers for such a revolution. This sensuality was meant to be expressed without shame or reservations. We have been silent and turned off far too long, completely intimidated and trumped by a sinister and perverted agenda; now is the time to speak, and allow God's intended and most intimate purpose to be lived out through our matrimonies.

The objective of this writing is to paint a transparent picture of our sensual purpose, for the sanctified to be satisfied and to replace the world's view of sex and sensuality with a view that won't make believers feel embarrassed or guilty about exploring or experiencing

one of Gods greatest gifts, INTIMACY in all of its varia-
tions and applications. This writing is a far cry from
being all inclusive but I believe it's a great place to get
the dialog started. My hope and prayer is that you would
have an open mind and a willing heart. I'm convinced
that men & women have distinctly different roles and
responsibilities in a relationship and that when these
differences are collaborated in concert can produce
mellifluous and lasting harmonies. There's no glass
ceiling in the bedroom, no good old boys or girls clubs;
we are on common and hallowed ground. So are you
ready for Undefiled Intimacy, Christianity between the
sheets? O.... . .then let the journey begin. Enjoy   and
may God bless you and yours!

Suggested material use

—〰—

*E*ach chapter can be dissected and digested in a confidential group setting to allow for thorough, objective and honest inputs and discussions or you may choose to dissect your marriage more privately (just the two of you). Either way, you decide your own level of participation, you may get more out of this than you may have initially considered. You choose. Most of all, **be honest**, you'd be surprised to find out that your sensual inquiries or frustrations have merit, are shared by your fellow brothers and sisters in Christ, and that God is aware of and cares about your sensual growth and fulfillment as a couple.

At the end of each chapter (beginning with chapter 3) I will challenge you with a scenario or with questions to discuss and/or to ponder. There is also a very pointed couple's questionnaire available in appendix A. I highly recommend trying to answer as much of the questions as possible as it relates to your particular situation. When sharing please proceed with wisdom a tender heart toward your mate.

Lastly, each chapter will be concluded with a short prayer. Let me reiterate that YOU decide your own level of involvement; but I dare you to get out of your 'sex box' and see what the Lord has waiting for you and your mate.

Introduction

—⚉—

Genesis 2:24

"For this reason (Marriage) a man shall leave his father and mother and be joined to his wife and the two shall become one flesh".

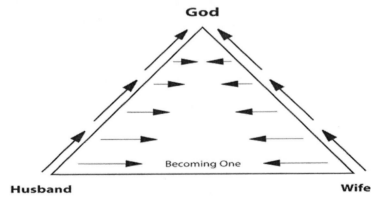

Marriage Takes Three

God

Becoming One

Husband   **Wife**

$\mathscr{N}$o matter how you slice it, marriage is work. It is labor intensive, takes a strong will and determination to last and should be, after our relationship with the Lord, be the most satisfying of all our relationships. To be very clear from the outset of this writing, it was and still is Gods idea and plan for you to become 'one flesh' with your spouse. This 'become' is an often arduous mandate and should be taken more seriously than many of us have taken it. This oneness, a lifetime transformation, includes spiritually, mentally, emotionally and yes, sensually. To become one requires deliberate effort, deliberate commitment, and deliberate consistency. As derived from this introductory scripture to 'become one' also co notates a gradual work in progress never fully coming to completion, never truly to arrive but to be in a perpetual state of evolution. This was a really exciting discovery for me. To know that we cannot exhaust the innumerable possibilities to become one with our spouses as we draw closer to God; we have the privilege of exploring one another over time and maturing in a way that can only be achieved through our sensual intimacy and fellowship. This sensuality is the glue that bonds our oneness; welcome to the rebirth of the bedroom!

Oftentimes I will use the term 'bedroom' as an overarching metaphor in lieu of a particular way (method) or particular location. Quite obviously love in the making can transpire in many places other than a bedroom and is not always a physical act; our daily fellowship and interaction with our significant other is all part of our intimacy as well. But it is the bedroom of our minds and the mental gymnastics we go through in trying to' be all that we can be' or failing to 'be all that we can be' to the opposite sex (our spouse) is what the focus of discussion is truly about. Allow me to also interject this point, you don't have to be Casanova's be deemed romantic, be yourself and allow God to use the personality He gave you to be romantic as you and your spouse define romance.

The intent is to be earnest in your efforts to rekindle the flames as you are graced to do so. Just remember to be open for changes and adjustments in your relationship as new opportunities arise. Moreover, understand that this is a journey and not necessarily a destination. Many years ago a former pastor and friend of mine told me that people can accomplish anything in life if they have a 'want to'. He'd say "you gotta have a Want To if you're going to get anything done in this life". That's where I am everyday with this and it has not been easy or without set backs. In spite of the challenges and failures we have all encountered, especially in our relationships, I still believe we should 'want to' become one, we should want to be the man or woman that God intended for us to be. Now what about you? By your reading of this material at the very least your curiosity is peaked, but how far are you willing to go.

Remember, your *'becoming'* is continuous and is a lifetime commitment so all excuses aside, do you have a want to? Are you really willing to get out of your comfort zone and address a very REAL issue that may be lurking in YOUR bedroom? Are you willing to humble yourself, perhaps even take your blinders off and admit that a true delinquency may exist? If not then you might want to stop reading now.

One of the purposes of this book is to provoke thought that will assist us in the sensual or sexual pursuit of our mates physically and emotionally. Undoubtedly, many of you will feel as if this is an inappropriate and unorthodox topic of discussion and believe me I understand your trepidation. Unfortunately, the topic of sensual intimacy has been so perverted that children of God rarely mention the word 'sex' in a positive context. You may not agree with everything stated within these pages but you cannot deny that there is a need in the Body of Christ for such candid discussion. More pointedly, there is a dire need in the church for saints to be open and honest about the condition of our bedrooms.

You may say it's a private matter but the reality is that what has been 'private' has been publicly destroying 'Christian' marriages and 'Christian' families for centuries Well, I'm calling on all these casualties to come out of the closet and get ministered to.

It is worth repeating at this juncture that I am addressing a specific audience, born again believers in Christ who know (or realize) that sensual intimacy in all its various forms and fashions is a gift from God and rightly belongs to us in the context of marriage. It is the Christian that should lead the sexual revolution, not secular media, not porn magazines or internet sites. You may consider some of these topics taboo, bodacious or even repulsive, that's OK; the church has been programmed to shy away from such sensitive topics. We have been conditioned for years to NOT talk about 'it' while we secretly sinned to satisfy our, God given, sensual urges. Shall we continue in this sin? Absolutely NOT! So, open your heart and mind and via the gift of the Holy Spirit let us proceed to comprehend with boldness what God is saying to us individually AND as a church on this issue. Let us take the appropriate measures, via active participation with our loved one, to get on the right track, reclaim what is rightfully our inheritance and then go forth and sin no more.

Chapter 1

An Epistle to Men

—⚏—

*O*h mighty men of valor, let me be the first to congratulate you for peeking into this book and considering the possibility that being intimate with your wife is more than what it has become. You may be a seasoned warrior in the corporate world, a champion in all sorts of sports and activities, yet you find yourself lacking at the place you call home. If we are going to make any significant and lasting progress in the arena of the bedroom then the time for making excuses must subside; we are men and we are to be the responsible shepherds of our homes.

Speaking of shepherds, there was this young man in the Old Testament who burst onto the scene like an unstoppable meteor and with his unseen authority accepted the challenge of the possibly 9ft tall mammoth from Gath. The young man was David and his foe, a descendent from giants, was Goliath. Never mind the fact that David was clearly the underdog, clearly out of his weight class, and clearly had a weapons disadvantage. Let's see a slingshot vs. a sword? The gamblers of the day were putting their money on a quick and decisive death to this ruddy looking shepherd boy. But their money would soon be lost because Goliath, in his arrogance and defiance, failed to consider the awesomeness of the God of Abraham, Isaac, Jacob and yes David

You probably already know the many stories of King David; he is one of my favorite personalities in scripture. He was handsome, he was a ladies man, he was a leader, he had influence, and he was talented. He was also brave and was clearly a man after Gods heart. He was by no means a perfect man, only Jesus was that, but David was passionate about everything he did. In the face of seemingly insurmountable challenges, he remained solid and undeterred. He was a man's man and keeping your intimacy in check is a man's work, it is not child's play or for prepubescent little boys; so be a man about it. Whether you are young or old, feeble or strong the Lord is with you to help you overcome all obstacles, even if the obstacle is Goliath or even if the obstacle happens to be you and your own stubbornness.

I know what it's like to have a woman drunk with passion and shivering with utter and complete satisfaction, it's a beautiful thing On the other hand, I also know what it is to feel as if you are making love to a frigid corpse. Even worse, I know what it feels like to not feel anything at all toward your spouse and sex has become mundane at best if it exists at all. Regrettably, many men assume that as long as they are satisfied (sensually) then their spouse must be satisfied as well. NOT the case! Nothing could be further from the truth. Your lady is not a video game that you can control or even predict; she is not a maid or servant that jumps at your beckon call and she is not your employee. She happens to be your God commissioned helper/companion, and as such is the most important woman in your world. We have failed to realize that when we are deficient in the 'bedroom' other areas of our lives and marriage become negatively affected as well (more on this later).

Intimacy or Sex talk is a touchy and sometimes uncomfortable subject to discuss (especially in the church) and not all men know how, or if they should, broach this sensitive subject with their significant other. Some men feel emasculated to find out that they aren't sensually as impressive as they imagined they were; so they'd rather not know at all; but withdrawal is not the answer either and doing so would only make matters worse. Also, as we age the desire and will to carry out our sensual calling changes, so we have to find *'other ways'* to demonstrate our intimacy. Some of us have just decided that all hope is lost and that there's nothing exciting about the bedroom and nothing romantic about romance; so we adjust and accept it as routine or normal, but what has it really cost us? Might I suggest that the 'romance factor' is not always about you and how YOU feel? What is HER definition of romance? Do you know?

I have also learned that sometimes love is not a 'feeling' at all but rather a **conscious decision** based on a **previous commitment**. Hmmm, let that sink in for a moment.

Gentlemen, we have to be more willing to compromise if we are going to have any hope of a happy and lasting relationship. Our ladies, like a delicate flower, are sensitive and we have to adapt to these sensitivities in order to maintain a healthy and thriving bedroom. It will take some work and some grand concessions on your part but a 'happy' home will make all your efforts pale in comparison. Be mindful that these compromises are out of your unconditional love for your sweetheart; so don't be abrasive about it and make her feel as if she is inconveniencing you. Some of you may even think that because you have been married to the same woman for decades there's no need in trying to re-capture the flames that once brought you together in the first place. Your wife may disagree.

So many Christian men are throwing in the towel on their bedrooms and obliviously leaving the door wide open for 'something else' to substitute their God ordained obligation. Believe me when I state that this 'substitute' can become a formidable adversary if left to fester the relationship. Again, keeping your intimacy undefiled is not for the faint of heart and it's not for milquetoast punks or chumps. It will take your continuous efforts, prayers and compassion but I believe that YOU are up to the task at hand. Like you, your wife has a sensual requirement that God placed in her being. She cannot be separated from hers any more than you can from yours and ignoring it does NOT get rid of it and just because you've been together for millennia doesn't mean it doesn't matter anymore either. My advice is that you don't ignore it but rather search it (intimacy) out and IGNITE it!

You shouldn't be intimidated by the gradual changes you and your spouse will experience over time as it pertains to your sensual wants and needs. On the contrary this should excite you! As the head of your household you will need to take the lead role and make your woman feel loved, safe, cherished and most of all DESIRED. In my observations and discussions through the years one theme is extremely common among wives (women) and that is that they yearn to be desired and to remain desirable, especially in the eyes of their husband. Another key I observed is that our ladies really want our attention; to ignore her is like committing a cardinal sin. One of our primary responsibilities, and challenges, as husbands is to keep our sensual desires FOCUSED on our wives and them alone.

There are all kinds of distractions out there specifically designed to keep us from our intimate calling in our marriages. Being primarily visually stimulated creatures, we are inundated with sensual imagery at every conceivable turn and if you're honest, you'll admit that many or most of these images blur the reality of what is your better half; no offense but the reality before you and the airbrushed hottie on your TV screen are quite different. This just adds to the confusion of the subject matter and although I do not claim to be an expert I do have some experiences and insights I'd like to share if you will allow me to, one Christian Brother to another.

In all honesty, I was VERY hesitant to accept this assignment and it took me years to actually put pen to paper. I kept brushing it off as nonsense but the more I brushed it off the more it was reinforced in my spirit and I felt like God was steering me to tell his body to wake up to this particular need of ministry. So, that's what it is my brother; it's a need in your relationship with your wife that will bring a new meaning to the word joy while bringing untold glory to God. He has given you this diamond in the rough that is your spouse and has placed in her everything you need to be intimately satisfied. EVERYTHING! No need to look any further. She is the complete and total package, programmed with needs and wants but it's up to you (as her lover, companion and partner) to pay attention to the instructions and signals she sends.

STOP being a selfish lover, if you are, and find out what makes her sensual clock tick, It's OK to ASK, and then set her alarm off on a regular basis. Quit complaining about what she doesn't do for you, whining does not become you, be the head of your home and set the tone by your actions and your love and consideration toward her. Do this with passion and machismo and watch a positive transformation come about. *"Husbands love your wives. . ."* that was the instructions to the church at Ephesus over two-thousand years ago and it's the same instructions we are called to adhere to today (see Ephesians 5:25). No excuses and no exceptions.

Think of the first time you saw her and dreamed of having her in your arms. Do you remember that? How about that first kiss and the head over heels feeling that overwhelmed you; do you remember that? Remember the aching feeling in your heart when you were apart and how you longed to be basking in her presence? Remember how protective you were of her and how you would have willingly given your life just to shield her from the slightest hint of harm. You clearly remember that, don't you? So, what happened? Time happened. Over time you (we) got way too cozy and familiar, and that cozy familiarity turned into complacency which turned us into bedroom casualties. Well it's not too late my friend there is hope that you can still regain your vigilance; be the 'hero' once again go ahead and get the dust off of your old Superman t-shirt, stick out your chest and rescue your woman and your bedroom will follow.

As men we naturally want to hunt, pursue, prowl and capture; now that we are married our objective should shift from getting her interested and satisfied to keeping her interested and satisfied; in return your desires will be met to the fullest. Oh, one more thing; if you or your spouse had done something to violate the trust between you, yet you have both taken it to the altar and have agreed to move on, then use this time to start anew in His grace. Believe it or not, God is just as interested and concerned with your sensual growth and maturity as He is with your spiritual and emotional growth with your wife. So keep praying about it together and relax, its ok to pursue her with a new set of eyes knowing God cares about your bedroom too regardless of how many years you have been married. It is my hope and prayer that you and your wife will be blessed by the candor on the pages that follow and that more importantly your marriage will be invigorated with ecstasy. Have fun, stay blessed and happy hunting.

Prayer:

Heavenly Father, you are our strength, our wisdom, understanding and might. There is none like you in all the infinite galaxies; you remain God of all. Help us mere men oh heavenly Savior, teach us via your word and Holy Spirit to become more than what we have thus far. We admit our failure to cover our wives with prayer and the love she so deserves. From this day forward I lean and depend on you to show me the error of my failed intimacy and will lean on your guidance to redirect my faith to reconnect in one purpose with my spouse. In Jesus name I thank you.

Amen

Chapter 2

An Epistle to Women

—ⱳⱳ—

Proverbs 31:10-12

*"Who can find a virtuous wife? For her **worth** is far*
above rubies**. The heart of her **husband** safely **trusts
***her**; so he will have **no lack** of gain. She does him*
***good** and **not evil** all the days of her life."*

*A*s you know ladies, there are many forms of intimacy; but for the primary purposes of this writing the terms of intimacy are referring to those actions of sensuality that are to be triggered and acted upon between a monogamous Christian husband and a monogamous Christian wife. You are who I had in mind in writing this book as I pondered the myriad mistakes, failures and outright catastrophes of my past relationships. Without question, these candid principles are to be shared and thoroughly enjoyed at your discretion by you and your spouse in complete trust, honesty and mutual agreement or consent.

Be forewarned, I am not a preacher, a noted scholar, and I do not have a PhD. in Sexology. What I bring to the discussion is not daunting wisdom of a relationship expert but rather the nearly three decades of trial by fire, bare knuckle and brutally honest relationship experience. I have no intention of vicariously interpreting the word of truth but will rather expound on what I have finally found to be practical gems of raw truth that has been key to keeping intimacy alive and thriving in and out of the bedroom. Moreover, I am just an average observer, and perhaps even a frustrated believer, answering a not so simple and yet compelling call. My deepest hope, agenda and practical advice to you is that you would take the time to diagnose the health of your intimacy and lower the risk of infidelity, estrangement or divorce.

Dear women of virtue, congratulations and thank you so very much for taking a moment to peruse these pages. This is a wonderful opportunity to pause, take notes and communicate in a loving way to your spouse how you truly feel about the intimate climate of the home you share. Not too long ago, as I was confiding with a married couple my thoughts on this book, the wife revealed to me that she had longed to be more 'expressive' with her husband in sensual matters but for many years thought that it would not be 'Christ like' to pursue such desires in her marriage. She said she felt 'dirty' about wanting to 'experiment' in order to spice up her marriage and thought her husband would resist her or be ashamed. Well, as I told her, that's just another lie from the enemy's camp and that it is precisely these types of thoughts and reservations that make our unions stale and wanting. Well guess what, as I told her, God has glamorous plans for you and your man starting tonight.

Don't be surprised, God is very concerned about your intimate and sensual satisfaction or lack thereof. For centuries women have been portrayed and exploited as just a 'piece of meat' and not much consideration was given to the intelligence of her wondrous mind, her genius, creativity and resourcefulness; even less consideration was given to her fulfillment or sensual satisfaction. Unfortunately, this demented attitude is still alive and well today even in modern societies like the United States of America. This was not Gods intent for one of his greatest creations. Your most intimate feelings are not frivolous, they matter to God.

Being intimate with your spouse doesn't have to be a drag or something that you presently abhor; you really shouldn't have to 'fake it' just to get him off of you. You and your husband have the right to be **equally** satisfied whether it's in the bedroom or simply holding hands as you walk down the street and you both have a calling or obligation to ensure that this mandate is carried out. It's truly the pleasure principle Gods way. Your hubby should take the lead but that doesn't mean that he always has to be the initiator, you can feel free to express your needs and desires to him knowing that he wants to make you happy while making your union holy.

Do not despair if it's been a while since you've experience a little bit of fireworks, give your man some time to adjust and be patient with his efforts. Consider his potential and how difficult it may be for him to regain, if just a vestige, of the momentum and 'machismo' he once had. Oh and one more very important thing, when addressing him, please practice restraint with the words you allow to project out of your mouth. Sarcasm is undoubtedly one of the most useful tools the devil uses to poison our unions, so don't feed the flames of that urge to demean or degrade your life partner. Instead speak blessings upon your hubby and curse him not. Speak and pray over him what you want him to become for you and never disrespect him or cut him down with ugly, potent and sharp words from your mouth (see Ephesians 5:33).

Take a pro-intimacy stance as you realize that your husband is an extension of you as you are an extension of him so speak to him as you want to be spoken to. Don't go around telling your girlfriends that your hubby is no good and that he's unromantic, lazy and worthless! Control that urge to let your tongue run off like an unrestrained sewer. What do you think your girlfriends see when they meet the man you call husband after you've degraded him so much? And please don't allow your BFF's (Best Friends Forever) to speak disparagingly about your man either. What you allow to come out of your mouth can be very potent and it's up to you to keep your girls in check when it comes to your God commissioned mate. Be extra careful to guard your relationship because not every woman that you tell about how good or bad things are can be relied on to support you; some are just conduits for hatred, envy and jealousy and their only joy comes from your despair.

"Behold, I send you out as sheep in the midst of wolves. Therefore be wise as serpents and harmless as doves."
(Mathew 10:16)

Remember, your man is a part of you and you both represent each other in Christ Jesus so wear Him well. If there were some trust issues in the past and you have both given it to God and agree to move forward with your relationship; then this is the perfect time to be open about what works in the bedroom and what doesn't work. Communication, compromise, and mutual under-standing and respect are paramount; especially in the bedroom where we are exposed and most vulnerable. Wouldn't you agree?

Keep praying about it together and remember you are the apple of your husbands' eye and he can't wait to make (and keep) you utterly satisfied with authentic delight. Go forth in the anointing of God, be naked and unashamed as you have fun reclaiming what is rightfully yours, SENSUAL healing unadulterated and undefiled.

Prayer

My Lord, my confidant and my friend, thank you for being so ever present and ever powerful. I know without a doubt that you love me and have my best interest at heart. Forgive me now for my the mismanagement of the intimacy between my spouse and I. His love and attention mean so much to me, I admit that I've acted out of my own insecurities and desires; please forgive and restore my heart and mind for your glory and the glory that my marriage represents. In Jesus name,

Amen

Chapter 3

Undefiled Defined

—⁓—

"Put on LOVE which is the PERFECT bond of UNITY."
(Colossians 3:14)

A ccording to the Encyclopedia Britannica, defiled is defined as to make unclean or impure: as (a) to corrupt the purity or perfection of or to debase; (b) to violate the chastity of: deflower (c) to make physically **unclean** especially with something **unpleasant** or **contaminating,** to **sully** and **dishonor.**

Most of us can relate to a time or season when we seemingly had more than our fair share of defilement. It could have been in the form of a cheating partner that not only bruised our relationship with unfaithfulness but demolished it with incessant lies. You know the kind, the lies that sound so eerily true that it gets you thinking that perhaps the whole debacle was your fault; the kind of lies that pierce with such precision that you wouldn't recognize the truth if it slammed into you with the force and impact of a freight train traveling at over 75 miles an hour. DEFILEMENT was the cry that started in the Garden of Eden back in antediluvian times, Genesis 3: 4-7, when Adam and Eve were deceived by the serpent and partook of the forbidden fruit.

"Then the serpent said to the woman, you will not surely die. For God knows that in the day you eat of it your eyes will be opened and you will be like God, knowing good and evil. So when the woman saw that the tree was good for food, that it was pleasant to the eyes, and a tree desirable to make one wise, she took of

its fruit and ate. She also gave to her husband with her, and he ate. Then the eyes of both of them were opened, and they knew that they were naked; and they sewed fig leaves together and made themselves coverings."

This deflowering of mankind back then seemed a permanent scar and would have been had it not been for the mercy of God and for the saving blood of His son, our Lord and Savior Jesus Christ. He who knew not sin became 'defiled' so that we could inherit once again an undefiled opportunity.

When something is Undefiled it is the complete opposite of the previously mentioned definitions. Let's use the opposite of definition (c) for example. To Undefile is to make physically clean, especially with something pleasant (*pleasure*) with NO contaminants, to praise and honor. Glory to God Hallelujah!! The writer of Hebrews tells us that the "marriage **BED** is **UNDEFILED**"!

<u>*Here are some undefiled Synonyms that may be helpful*</u>: *blameless, crimeless, decent, exemplary, faultless, good, guiltless, honorable, inculpable, innocent, modest, moral, respectable, sinless, unsullied, upright, wholesome. . .*

This is the only place in scripture (KJV) where 'undefiled' is used in the context of marital intimacy. This is so praise worthy! I don't know what you thank God for but I highly recommend adding sensual intimacy to the list of the top ten things you thank God for☺.

We thank Him for food, shelter, money, our loved ones, friends, etc. etc. etc. and rightly so. We hear sermons every week that exhort us to be thankful but when was the last time you heard a sermon about thanking God for our sensual side? Well, God invented sex and all the trimmings of our sensuality that's associated with it. Engaging in this activity physically, emotionally, and spiritually was designed to be extremely enjoyable and gratifying for both the man AND the woman! If so, then we need to add sensuality to our list of thanks and praise to the Lord.

Are you willing to entertain a new way of thinking about your sensuality? Haven't you heard that when the praises go up, the blessings come down? Well it's time to get your praise on for intimacy and let the blessings come down and literally stimulate new life into your sheets.

It's really going to be up to you and your spouse to scrupulously accept or reject the opportunity to rekindle the flames of passion and keep the sensual embers burning. I hope you elect to pursue this God ordained activity and re-connect with your spouse in new and inventive ways; I dare you to go forth and let your bedroom become the most anointed and most exciting room in the house. If you haven't figured it out yet, this is not *necessarily* about the great commission, to go forth preaching, teaching etc. to get people saved. You should ALREADY be saved; **this material is not about the salvation of your soul but about the salvation of your bedroom.**

Jesus told his disciples throughout John chapters 14 & 15 that He would send the Holy Spirit and that the Holy Spirit would bring things to our remembrance and would guide us into ALL truth. What is the 'truth' about the sensual climate in your home? What is the truth about your MUTUAL and unselfish satisfaction? What is the truth about your sensual intentions? Not only can the Holy Spirit help us but this *"Teacher"* has an obligation, during this finite dispensation of grace, to provide us sensual insight into how to please our mates and how to KEEP them pleased over time as we transition through this most fragile and temporal thing called life.

Don't let Him off the hook either; He is eager to assist us if we would but ask. As we will discuss later,

God has a vested interest in your marital obedience and satisfaction because it represents a much larger picture, His holiness is on display and you and I are the beneficiaries of His sensual magnificence.

"If there is anything praise worthy. . .

think (meditate) on these things"

(Philippians 4:8)

Couple discussion:

- How do you define 'Undefiled' as it relates to the author of Hebrews?

- How could undefiled intimacy relate to the Great commission?

- Do you believe the Holy Spirit has an obligation to and is willing to instruct us in the areas of intimacy with our spouses? How so?

- Have you ever felt dirty or guilty about lusting after your spouse in a certain way? Care to share?

- Would you agree with your spouse that you share a 'mutually' satisfying sensual relationship? Dare to share?

Prayer:

Heavenly Father, we humble ourselves before you at this time and ask that you renew our minds according to your perfect will in this endeavor. Open our hearts and ears to hear what Your Spirit has to say about the condition of our most sacred and private space. Help me as a husband/wife to be willing and able to do and be whatever it takes to keep our marital union happy, holy and undefiled. I thank you in advance for what you're doing and for what you are about to do in our ever maturing relationship. In Jesus name Amen.

Chapter 4

Confronting the bedroom (Sex wars exposed)

—ɯ—

"Let your fountain be blessed; and **rejoice** *with the wife of your youth. Let her be as the loving hind and pleasant roe; let her breast* **satisfy you** *at all times and be thou* **ravished** *always with her love. And why will you, my son, be ravished with a strange woman, and embrace the bosom of a stranger?"*

(Proverbs 5: 18-20, emphasis mine)

S preading the gospel message that Jesus the Christ came to this earth as God robbed in flesh to die for the sins of man, was buried and rose on the third day in eternal victory is our primary and undeniable mission as Christians. Salvation can be found in no other than Christ our Lord, for the ONLY way to get to the Father is thru the Son. This redemption of souls and bringing God glory is what we strive for in all our service in Christ, regardless of our specific calling. However, without discipleship our ministries would not be as fruitful or as productive as it was intended to be. We all need grooming, a mentor, someone who can provide a consistent positive and stimulating influence in our lives. With the right tools, application and accountability this stimulus can move us to purpose and productivity.

"There are diversities of gifts, but the same Spirit. There are differences of ministries, but the same Lord. And there are diversities of activities, but it is the same God who works all in all. But the manifestation of the Spirit is given to each one for the profit of all."

(1 Corinthians 12: 4-7)

Joshua was groomed as he followed Moses; Elisha was groomed as he followed Elijah and so on. Even the apostle Paul said "follow me as I follow Christ". As previously stated, this book was not written to get people saved, it is written to encourage vigilance, to disciple, revive, empower and keep already saved and married couples unified through the power and authority of sensual intimacy.

Our home is the first place we receive our nourishment to spread the gospel and it's where we first put into practice the principles we learn in scripture. Home is where those closest to us see our true colors and they have the awesome audacity to praise our progress and delicately scrutinize or critique our failures. Someone once said that "home is where the heart is", it's where we can let our hair down and have a feeling of security in ourselves and in those we share this exquisite space with. The last place we should feel timid, unloved and ashamed is in our own home and the last place we should feel degraded or emasculated is in the comfort of our castle.

More pointedly, there's not much else that can strike a blow to a man or woman's self esteem or self worth than a failed evaluation of bedroom prowess and etiquette. This is an unequivocal fact; no need to argue this point, there is no debating required. When our significant others are dissatisfied with our bedroom antics and they become saddened, nauseated, and repulsed at the thought of being intimate with us, it affects everything else in our lives. **Nothing wounds our emotions or cuts us more deeply than an unfulfilled partner**. Whether you say amen or not, you know that's the truth so need for the shocked look on your face.

Generally speaking, Christian couples who aren't intimate with their spouses, or have gradually declined in the affection department, usually pour themselves into other areas of work or ministry. Or, they start to stay longer at work, stay longer at the gym, and take the long way home so they can claim they're exhausted when they finally get there. They may even pretend not to see you when you're naked because perhaps you packed on a few pounds or your constant nagging and negative attitude make you unsightly or less than desirable. Or perhaps they avoid being naked around you altogether for similar reasons. They (which could be any of us) simply try to ignore the reality of the situation, embracing the denial because it's less painful to accept. They try to live as if all is well when the opposite is a more accurate depiction. No one wants to deal with this awkwardness head on so we ignore it, and all it does is—grow.

But what does 'it' grow into? You can be in defiance if you want to but the bedroom knows the ugly truth about you. Your marriage bed is keeping meticulous records of your absence and your failure to fulfill your sensual calling. You may try to discount it by keeping a busy schedule, but that lie will never satisfy and only the truth will ever really set you free from this self-imposed prison. Your spouse knows the real you, the man or woman of God who hides because of their own insecurities. The spouse who can please everyone else, can make time for everyone else, can make everyone else happy, can make everyone else smile, everyone else feel listened to, loved and special; everyone but their own wife or husband.

The writer of Proverbs five stated that we should be satisfied and ravished with one another and asks a crucial question "why should we be ravished by a stranger". Who is this stranger? Could he or she be the activities we lend ourselves to? Could this stranger be comfort food, or incessant shopping? Could this stranger be good deeds done at a bad time or the right seed planted in the wrong season? Think about it. You may volunteer to assist on this or that committee or you go from sermon to sermon, conference to conference, and revival to revival in complete and utter oblivion. You may even be secretly attached to a television show, the internet, or sports! Again, I ask, who is this stranger? Who or what stole your attention from your mate? Why has intimacy declined? You are called husband, wife, CEO, manager, pastor, bishop, missionary, evangelist, elder, deacon, usher, choir director, prophet or whatever other title you want to be called; but your spouse calls you a flake, a phony and a delinquent!

Are you ravishing strangers? Are you unaware of the timing and needs of your mate? You may even sleep in a separate bedroom thinking that this is a suitable solution adamantly claiming that this is the only way to keep the peace at home; but you are only fooling yourself as this only adds to the problem. What you are really doing is sustaining a war! You can run, and you can hide but sooner or later you must settle the score with your sheets. Be encouraged my friend, you can change this! You possess the power to reverse the damage that has been done and to reclaim what was lost. Not only can you reverse this downward spiral but you have the potential to make things in your relationship better than they ever were before. I believe that things don't have to stay the way they are, the Holy Spirit waits to assist; better days are yet before you but first you must go home and confront the bedroom!

The costs of these bed wars are astronomical and the casualties are mounting more and more each day; if there is going to be a cessation of these hostilities then someone is going to have to humble themselves in order to regain control of these frantic and undisciplined sheets.

"Behold, you are handsome my beloved!
Yes pleasant. Also, our bed is green (ready).
Song of Solomon 1: 16.

Pardon the imposition but when was the last time you had a mind blowing sensual experience together? Think about the last time you and your spouse had an equally satisfying sensual experience. How long has it been? Now consider your most recent sensual experience, how was 'it' attained? Do the bed wars continue? Was it arduous labor where you had to work extra hard to 'get it' like an earned vacation or was it like getting a reward for taking out the trash or doing the dishes? Did you have to earn it like a 'good puppy' or was it like a miracle that you could get it up and that she would actually allow you entry? Silly sheets, those tricks are for kids.

If your present situation is something like one of the above mentioned scenarios then you really need this literature. Don't get me wrong, I do believe we should take time to partake in our church ministries and soul saving activities; but I believe in doing so with moderation and wisdom. If my home is in disarray and my sheets are depleted than I believe my first focus and calling is to take care of my household; after Christ my wife comes first, period. Our first witness is to our loved ones.

"But if anyone does not provide for his own, and especially for those of his household, he has denied the faith and is worse than an unbeliever." (1 Timothy 5:8)

I grew up in Brooklyn New York in a single parent home. My parents had separated and divorced before I was a teenager and I don't recall, when they were married or afterward, ever having any conversations or guidelines from them about the 'birds and the bees'. My mother is an amazing woman; I call her my she-hero or 'shero' because she had the courage to leave my abusive alcoholic father after many years of an unloving relationship. The good news is that God has restored to her for the years she was unloved and abused with an extraordinary new husband who is loyal, romantic and treats my mother like the queen she is. They are celebrating 25+ years together as of the writing of this book. Anyway, as I was saying I had not been indoctrinated in the proper ways of 'boy meeting girl'. So, in my younger years, and well before accepting Christ into my life, I remember how me and my guy friends would scheme and strategize various methods to flatter the ladies into 'letting us' get into their panties. Back then we would do and say just about anything to 'get laid'.

We were foolish adolescent novices influenced primarily by TV and aroused by the slightest glimpse into a porn magazine. We were also influenced by the local hoodlums and street savvy pimps who were always more than willing to 'share' their unsolicited and perceived expertise in womanizing. We were like amateur lawyers presenting a case as to why we were deserving of the female anatomy. We honed our skills and relished in every opportunity to dazzle the ladies with our pathetic bravado. Even when we feigned tough and disinterest, no matter how strong we thought we were, her 'coochie' (urban colloquialism for vagina) was like kryptonite and we were incapable to resist her. I recall corny lines like 'hey girl, you know you want to give me some of that good stuff' or 'baby you look so fine I would gladly drink your bath water'. Yeah I know VERY corny. Anyway, the response I would typically get was 'I aint givin you none' or 'you aint getting none of this', although being the persistent type that I was, I'd end up 'getting' some of what she said that she wasn't giving. As I grew older, and somewhat wiser, I came across more 'aggressive' women and realized that 'she' wanted it as much as I did but went about getting it quite differently.

And so began my distorted comprehension that sex had to be 'earned' and that females contained special super powers to manipulate and grant or deny me access to their cherished anatomy. The 'mighty coochie' befell many of my adolescent comrades and I thought I was powerless despite my own verbal exploitation and assumed that men always wanted to have sex with women and that women only 'occasionally' wanted to have sex with men depending upon what they could 'get' from them. Growing up believing that in order to 'get some' I had to perform a variety of tasks or assignments was faulty and dysfunctional thinking. Unfortunately I am not alone. I have discovered that this mental sex battle is thriving; it is alive and well in the church of the living God.

To me it was as if the female was the sole proprietor of sensual intimacy and was only going to engage (or give it up) as a favor to the male. I was so clueless and out of tune; it seemed as if her mesmerizing vagina was wielded as a powerful tool of manipulation instead of a tool to enhance a godly relationship. Her hips, lips and fingertips were my consistent undoing. One day out of the blue, I noticed during my sexcapades that she was truly 'getting' something out of the deal as well, on many occasions much more than I. Suddenly my paradigm began to shift and I realized that I had incorrect information about intimacy and what it was meant to be. This misinformation puzzled me for years until I got saved and dared to pray about it and ask questions from those I considered much wiser than myself. I don't claim to be completely there yet but thank God I'm not where I used to be.

Sadly, many believers today still fall prey to this destructive style of 'sex for sale'; it's literally akin to harlotry whereby our own marital union is devalued, cheapened and degraded. The big 3 (which will be discussed in chapter 7), emotional connection, stimulation and mutual satisfaction is for the wife AND the husband. Sex should never be used as an ultimatum or a bargaining chip. Gods' intent was never meant for sex to be quid pro quo. When a spouse, whether out of anger, spite or ignorance, declares 'you aint getting none' that's an outright declaration of WAR and they are bringing shame to the union and actually depriving themselves of 'becoming' as well.

As I was watching TV the other day a Jack in the Box commercial came on. Jack was playing Scrabble with his wife and came up with a word that apparently was worth a lot of points. He was so excited to have come up with such a clever and robust combination of letters. To his wife's dismay she retorted with another word and a not so obvious message to Jack. Her word was 'nonookie'. Secular society has this on lock! At first Jack was puzzled and asked his wife "what's that mean?" she uttered not a word but rather provided a satirical facial expression. "Oh" was Jacks impotent response. I know it's just supposed to be a comical commercial, but to me the undertone of the message is a revolting reminder that our sensual vigilance can never go on vacation.

Over time such sexual manipulation builds up an arsenal of negative emotions and utter disconnection in the marital relationship. So confront your bedroom and take a stand! Don't be like Jack and just respond with "Oh☹", if you don't get any then she doesn't get any either right? It's a foolish and futile game. When this happens time and time again, the bond and unity begins to crumble; becoming one is put on pause. Remember, your sex and sensuality toward her is just as important as her sex and sensuality is to you. In this we are equal there are no winners in sex wars only losers. Furthermore, such **performance based sex**, over time, can make an already poor relationship even worse. So what do we do? We continue to fill our calendars with activities that may be taking the place of moments of intimacy we could be sharing with our spouse.

It's like we aren't even paying attention to the subtleties that creep in overtime and slowly but surely stain our relationships with Sinicism, sarcasm and busyness. Some level of wooing is expected on both sides as it pertains to setting the mood and disarming the stresses but not to the point of intentional manipulation. I believe that married men of God want to be faithful and want to have their spouse meet and/or exceed their every fantasy and vice versa; so why is it that so many of us have failed so miserably in the bedroom? Could it be our distorted notions of what sex is and is NOT supposed to be? Could it be that what we thought we 'owned' isn't really ours at all? We will explore the concept of 'ownership' later when we get to the book of Corinthians.

Check out this manipulative example from scripture where today we would clearly define it as sexually charged and manipulative situation. Genesis 30:14-16: New International Version (NIV), (Emphasis mine).

14. During wheat harvest, Reuben went out into the fields and found some mandrake plants, which he brought to his mother Leah. Rachel said to Leah, "Please give me some of your son's mandrakes."

15. But she said to her, "Wasn't it enough that you took away my husband? Will you take my son's mandrakes too?"

*"Very well," Rachel said, "he (Jacob their shared husband) can sleep with you tonight **in return** for your son's mandrakes."*

*16. So when Jacob came in from the fields that evening, Leah went out to meet him. "You **must** sleep with me," she said. "I have **hired you** with my son's mandrakes." So he slept with her that night.*

Jacob (Israel) had two notable wives, Leah and Rachael. Leah did not feel as if she was loved by Jacob despite having giving birth to most of his children {Note: Intimacy is more than just sex}. In this particular text, she was so jealous of her younger sister Rachael having the love and attention of Jacob that she agreed to a deal with her to buy Jacob for the evening to make Jacob sleep with her. Jacob was pimped by Rachael to his other manipulative wife but this did not make him love or appreciate Leah any more. Apparently Leah thought that having more kids or more sex would make Jacob desire her more, but it did not.

Some of you ladies may be asking 'what about the husbands role in being manipulative'? Good question. Either way is unhealthy and unproductive; whether it's using your body as a negotiating tool or allowing yourself to become so involved in activities that you are simply not available. Either method can cause estrangement. One day you will wake up only to find that you have been sharing your bed with a complete stranger and the time you have wasted can NEVER be recovered. So confront your bedroom! The bottom line is that either party can manipulate the other into getting what they want in exchange for intimate attention or they can make their spouse feel as if they have to 'earn' the right to share the bedroom. Such manipulation is flat out wrong and will lead to sexual dysfunction, frustration, estrangement and resentment. The devil would like nothing more than to keep these hostilities thriving in the most intimate place in our homes. . .the bedroom!

But wait, there is much more rewarding alternative; this is a more fruitful and gratifying alternative, ***Relationship based intimacy.*** Relationship based intimacy does not require a forced, faked or otherwise manipulative performance from either party. This type of intimacy is AGAPE driven, whereby a man and his wife (and wife AND her husband) WANT to GIVE of themselves to each other with no strings attached (NSA). This is the kind of affection that looks past those extra pounds and sees the beautiful person you have always been to them; this agape intimacy looks for ways to make you feel loved more today than you were loved yesterday.

This agape intimacy holds your hand when you walk down the street and couldn't care less who sees it. This relationship based intimacy spoons you tight way into the midnight hour and this agape intimacy is vigilant to confront the bedroom with regularity. Keep in mind that relationship based intimacy is a pleasant journey not a hurried destination. So, regardless of how good you think you are in the intimacy department, you must be willing to adapt to your spouse's changing needs overtime. Herein lies wisdom, patience and lots and lots of practice☺.

In this ideal setting you both want to be satisfied with every facet that leads up to the sexual activity and take deliberate actions to ensure that the other is fulfilled also. In this scenario, the lines of communication are clear and you both have the unequivocal assurance that you can be naked and not be ashamed.

"Be of the same mind toward one another"

(Romans 12:16)

With agape intimacy your mate gradually becomes the entire focal point of your every kinky thought and fantasy. This is the kind of daydreaming that you don't have to feel guilty about or feel as if you have to repent for doing or thinking something perverted. It's ok to lust after your spouse, it's ok to try a new position, it's ok to be creative, it's ok to get 'freaky' (or not) in your undefiled bedroom! This is the freedom we have unashamedly as believers as we reclaim this God given privilege of intimacy. Go ahead and hug or take a walk while you hold hands. Isn't it time you took back command of your bedroom and rebuked that boring, lethargic spirit that's been nestled in your sheets for far too long? Yes, I think so.

<u>Be forewarned</u>: Confronting the bedroom won't be easy if you have years of sensual decay built up in your relationship: not to mention, again, that the devil doesn't want you to get your bedroom mojo back! Satanic persuasions would like nothing more than for us to stay in the dark on the subject of sensual enjoyment and fulfillment. Satan would just love for us to keep looking to porn, prostitutes and seductive television programming for our sexual fixes and answers. He'd like us to keep thinking that sex is a 'dirty word' used by perverts and that intimate discussions are personal and have no place in the church. Mostly, he'd like you to keep being sensually unsatisfied with your spouse so perhaps you'd consider getting your pleasures elsewhere. Well, we all know what the devil is right? HE'S A LIAR!

My friends hear me out; God gets the glory out of your thriving relationship with each other. It's no surprise why God said in Genesis 2:18 *"It is not good that man should be alone; I will make him a helper comparable to him."* Your union is symbolic of Christ and his radiant bride the church. Good loving at home makes your radiance shine at work; shine at play, shine at school, shine as you shop and so on. The glow of being loved and loving completely will make sinners want what you have and will make other believers curious and want to know more about their inheritance. So let's confront our bedrooms and keep the light shinning!

Some of you can relate to this; I have been to a myriad of church services where I heard the preacher declare emphatically that there is power in the spoken word. A preacher would rightly say things like 'speak the word over your children and cover them with the blood of Jesus' or 'tell that devil to get his hands off of your finances' or more directly I'd hear them say 'Satan I rebuke you in the name of Jesus Christ and I command you to leave. . .'. I highly recommend (and I say this with the utmost conviction) that we finally confront the bedroom and speak to our sheets, pillows, blankets and mattress that Satan has no place in there.

Rebuke him from your bedroom with the authority of Jesus Christ and plead the blood over your sensual revolution. While you are at it allow me to interject this sobering statement: Do not wait until your spouse has some type of debilitating illness like breast cancer or testicular cancer before you start to pray over their body parts. Pray over each other's anatomy NOW!

Touch the breast of your wife and thank God for them, anoint each other from head to toe thanking God for her feminine parts, bless the Lord for lips, hips, and finger-tips. Ladies thank God for your husband's masculinity, for his strong embrace. Thank God for the privilege of simply holding hands or being able to caress and hold one another.

Please consider this sobering story from an unknown author:

". . .When I got home that night as my wife served dinner, I held her hand and said, I've got something to tell you. She sat down and ate quietly. Again I observed the hurt in her eyes.

Suddenly I didn't know how to open my mouth. But I had to let her know what I was thinking. I want a divorce. I raised the topic calmly. She didn't seem to be annoyed by my words, instead she asked me softly, why?

I avoided her question. This made her angry. She threw away the chopsticks and shouted at me, you are not a man! That night, we didn't talk to each other. She was weeping. I knew she wanted to find out what had happened to our marriage. But I could hardly give her a satisfactory answer; she had lost my heart to Bethany. I didn't love her anymore. I just pitied her!

With a deep sense of guilt, I drafted a divorce agreement which stated that she could own our house, our car, and 40% stake of my company. She glanced at it and then tore it into pieces. The woman who had spent ten years of her life with me had become a stranger. I felt sorry for her wasted time, resources and energy but I could not take back what I had said for I loved Bethany so dearly. Finally she cried loudly in front of me, which was what I had expected to see. To me her cry was actually a kind of release. The idea of divorce which had obsessed me for several weeks seemed to be firmer and clearer now.

The next day, I came back home very late and found her writing something at the table. I didn't have supper but went straight to sleep and fell asleep very fast because I was tired after an eventful day with Bethany. When I woke up, she was still there at the table writing. I just did not care so I turned over and was asleep again.

In the morning she presented her divorce conditions: she didn't want anything from me, but needed a month's notice before the divorce. She requested that in that one month we both struggle to live as normal a life as possible. Her reasons were simple: our son had his exams in a month's time and she didn't want to disrupt him with our broken marriage.

This was agreeable to me. But she had something more, she asked me to recall how I had carried her into out bridal room on our wedding day. She requested that every day for the month's duration I carry her out of our bedroom to the front door ever morning. I thought she was going crazy. Just to make our last days together bearable I accepted her odd request.

I told Bethany about my wife's divorce conditions. . She laughed loudly and thought it was absurd. No matter what tricks she applies, she has to face the divorce, she said scornfully.

My wife and I hadn't had any body contact since my divorce intention was explicitly expressed. So when I carried her out on the first day, we both appeared clumsy. Our son clapped behind us, daddy is holding mommy in his arms. His words brought me a sense of pain. From the bedroom to the sitting room, then to the door, I walked over ten meters with her in my arms. She closed her eyes and said softly; don't tell our son about the divorce. I nodded, feeling somewhat upset. I put her down outside the door. She went to wait for the bus to work. I drove alone to the office.

On the second day, both of us acted much more easily. She leaned on my chest. I could smell the fragrance of her blouse. I realized that I hadn't looked at this woman carefully for a long time. I realized she was not young any more. There were fine wrinkles on her face, her hair was graying! Our marriage had taken its toll on her. For a minute I wondered what I had done to her.

On the fourth day, when I lifted her up, I felt a sense of intimacy returning. This was the woman who had given ten years of her life to me. On the fifth and sixth day, I realized that our sense of intimacy was growing again. I didn't tell Bethany about this. It became easier to carry her as the month slipped by. Perhaps the everyday workout made me stronger.

She was choosing what to wear one morning. She tried on quite a few dresses but could not find a suitable one. Then she sighed, all my dresses have grown bigger. I *suddenly realized that she had grown so thin, that was the reason why I could carry her more easily.*

Suddenly it hit me. . . she had buried so much pain and bitterness in her heart. Subconsciously I reached out and touched her head.

Our son came in at the moment and said, Dad, it's time to carry mom out. To him, seeing his father carrying his mother out had become an essential part of his life. My wife gestured to our son to come closer and hugged him tightly. I turned my face away because I was afraid I might change my mind at this last minute. I then held her in my arms, walking from the bedroom, through the sitting room, to the hallway. Her hand surrounded my neck softly and naturally. I held her body tightly; it was just like our wedding day.

But her much lighter weight made me sad. On the last day, when I held her in my arms I could hardly move a step. Our son had gone to school. I held her tightly and said, I hadn't noticed that our life lacked intimacy. I drove to office. . . . jumped out of the car swiftly without locking the door. I was afraid any delay would make me change my mind. . .I walked upstairs. Bethany opened the door and I said to her, Sorry, Bethany, I do not want the divorce anymore.

She looked at me, astonished, and then touched my forehead. Do you have a fever? She said. I moved her hand off my head. Sorry, Bethany, I said, I won't divorce. My marriage life was boring probably because she and I didn't value the details of our lives, not because we didn't love each other anymore. Now I realize that since I carried her into my home on our wedding day I am supposed to hold her until death does us apart.

Bethany seemed to suddenly wake up. She gave me a loud slap and then slammed the door and burst into tears. I walked downstairs and drove away. At the floral shop on the way, I ordered a bouquet of flowers for my wife. The salesgirl asked me what to write on the card. I smiled and wrote, I'll carry you out every morning until death do us apart.

That evening I arrived home, flowers in my hands, a smile on my face, I ran upstairs, only to find my wife in the bed -dead. My wife had been fighting CANCER for months and I was so busy with Bethany to even notice. She knew that she would die soon and she wanted to *save me from whatever negative reaction from our son, in case we push through with the divorce. — At least, in the eyes of our son — I'm a loving husband. . . .*

The small details of your lives are what really matter in a relationship. It is not the mansion, the car, property, the money in the bank. These create an environment conducive for happiness but cannot give happiness in themselves.

So find time to be your spouse's friend and do those little things for each other that build intimacy. If you are not in a relationship now, remember this for the second (or third) time around. It's never too late."

I wept after I read this and then I got angry and rushed back to try to finish writing this book. Our Christian lights should be shining in our marriages and I want to do my part to warn believers of the danger of assuming that our intimacy is OK. Don't assume ASK, PRAY and take action to make certain that your intimacy is safeguarded, vibrant and healthy until death do you part. I say again, God is concerned about your bedroom but we have failed to study to show ourselves approved unto Him in this area. If our failure in the

bedroom can cause an avalanche of appalling consequences and experiences then wouldn't the opposite be
true if we have victory in our bedrooms?

Absolutely! There are untold benefits to having a
better bedroom. The marriage bed is a sacred place, it
is hallowed ground and set aside for the believers use.
Your marital stewardship will be judged with more
harshness than other areas of stewardship. Your relationship with your spouse is exceedingly prized above
other family members, material possessions, friends, or
co-workers.

My dear brothers and sisters, I would be remiss
in closing this chapter without asking you this. What
makes our *spiritual battle* different from secular society?
Quite obviously our risen and eternally victorious
Savior, but also our support systems as heirs of Christ
are unparalleled.

2 Corinthians 10: 4 & 5 reads *"For the weapons of our
warfare are not carnal but mighty in God for pulling
down strongholds, casting down arguments and every
high thing that exalts itself against the knowledge of*

God, bringing every thought into captivity to the obedience of Christ."

If you had at your disposal an arsenal of weaponry how would you respond to someone if they were to attempt to physically harm or attack your spouse? I think it's safe to assume that we would use anything at our disposal to protect and defend our loved ones, but when it comes to spiritual defense there are some 'soft targets' that I'm convinced that we give the enemy the advantage. How so? Well for example, if I were a betting man I'd bet that when we stop pursuing each other we are letting our guards down, when we use our bodies as manipulative tools we are letting our guards down and as a result our relationships take a 'hit' from the enemy. Over time these become strongholds and chip away at our armor and the demise of our intimacy is imminent. Confronting our bedrooms and being consistently attentive will keep our intimacy armed and battle ready!

Here are some other possible strongholds that you may have not considered as enemies to intimacy:

- Unrepentant sin
- Un-forgiveness

- Sarcasm
- Unbelief
- Stubbornness
- Denial
- Blame
- Selfishness
- Self-pity
- Anger
- Self-deceit
- Spiritual malnourishment
- Procrastination
- Mental infidelity

With this book we dare to launch out into the deep on a topic that rarely gets mentioned across pulpits all over the globe no matter what day of the week the church doors are open. Like a soul gone astray we intend to PULL your dead or dying sex life out of the PIT; we intend to provoke the passion and season the sheets with newfound flavor. This buffet in the bedroom will prove the scriptures and affirm Gods command to *"be fruitful and multiply" (Genesis 1: 22)*. He had more than breeding in mind then and He has more than breeding in mind now, but you must first confront your bedroom. Get to it!

Couple discussion:

- Do you feel as if there is an invisible enemy is your bedroom? How so?

- What type of changes do you need to make (if any) to your attitude or to your daily routine to be a more vigilant lover?

- Has your sex been used as a manipulative tool? If so how has this effected your relationship?

- How many rewards of relationship based intimacy can you come up with?

- Discuss how you can be more of a 'radiant' example to others.

- Discuss what you think some soft targets are in your relationship and how you can defend against them.

- What can you or should you start doing today to show more appreciation for your spouse.

Prayer:

Heavenly Father, I thank you in all things and I pray that you would especially cover our intimate relation-ships with your pure and precious love. Forgive us for all the times we failed to present our bodies to You and our spouses as the living sacrifice that You have called for. I pray that You would renew our hearts and minds in this endeavor so that we can go forward restored and refreshed. Strengthen us to maintain consistency and vigilance so we can be aware of the enemy's attempts to threaten our intimacy in Jesus name, Amen.

Chapter 5

Ministry of Ministries
(The Ministry of Intimacy)

—ᴍ—

*And He Himself gave some to be apostles, some
prophets, some evangelists, and some pastors and
teachers, for the equipping of the saints for the work of
ministry, for the edifying of the body of Christ, till we all
come to the unity of the faith and of the knowledge of
the Son of God, to a perfect man, to the measure of the
stature of the fullness of Christ;" (Ephesians 4: 11-13).*

*I*n any ministry it matters what you say and how
you say it; it matters what you pray and how your
heart prays it. Marriage is work just like any other
ministry yet I have noticed among many of my friends
and associates signs that they have stopped working

on their marriages. The signs are obvious and in broad daylight. We can see the turbulence in their cold and callous actions toward one another. The world is acutely aware that their relationship is on 'autopilot' and one of the dangers of an autopilot marriage is that it fails to adjust to changes in the heading but rather resist the change to stay 'on course'. Irrespective of the boisterous winds tugging, pulling and pushing the relationship to new heights and unexplored territory that stubborn autopilot brings it right back to where it used to be and an opportunity for new joy is squandered.

The giddiness early on in our marriages matures into something more fulfilling as we develop and grow in our love for each other; if one of us remains on autopilot we will miss this transformation. We can't stay stuck in the past of what used to be the 'good old days' constantly reminiscing about the ways we were. Our relationships require a particular stamina and vigilance in order to get from one stage of love and romance to the next. Certainly there's nothing wrong with being nostalgic for the sake of nostalgia but not for the sake of keeping our unions in perpetual adolescence.

There's no easy way to say this so I'll just say it, we get lazy and stop trying to impress and impart love that is almost often in flux. Cozy familiarity strikes over and over again until the damage done is almost irreversible. This happened to me, I only thought about my feelings and how inconvenienced I was. Selfishly I continued to ignore the obvious signs of change, in order to remain in my 'comfort zone', and that was the beginning of the end of my marriage.

Ask any pastor how their ministry is doing or what the 'climate' is of the flock in which they Sheppard and they will likely give you an earful of surface issues that are a part of church business. They will likely talk about building projects, tithing issues, supporting missions, employee or volunteer status and the like. Ask an evangelist about evangelical stuff and they likely will fill your ears with stories about revival throughout the land and how God is performing outright miracles everyday all over the world. Ask the prophet, the apostle, the bishop or the teacher and likewise you will get an abundance of information that pertains to the 'moving' of God in their particular ministry or calling. It's a beautiful thing and I praise God with all my heart for His many blessings in so many different areas and walks of life. The scriptures tell us that we don't all have the same ministry or calling but we all have the same spirit who leads and guides according to His perfect will, His glory and His pleasure.

Now back to this peculiar ministry; we readily boast about church growth and beam about plans and programs to promulgate the gospel. Praise the Lord; this is a great and marvelous thing. However, ask these same ministers about their sex lives and about the sensual health or climate of the married members in their congregation and you may be shocked at the response, if you get a response at all. Don't get discouraged; just know that the same Helper (Holy Spirit) that equips us to live obedient and godly lives can also help us to be just as fruitful in the ministry of our sensuality. And YES it is a valid inquiry.

We have often seen and experienced tremendous successes in our walks with God through the ministries He has entrusted to us. This is indisputably the will of God and may He continue to bless us in these endeavors. But, do we see and experience this same progressive success in our intimacy? An honest answer would likely be no. Under the anointing, the proverbial spout where the glory comes out, we preach, teach, evangelize, and prophesy to a few, a dozen or hundreds of millions yet an un-defiled bedroom shared by two is left un-ministered to and un-prayed for. What's up with that?

It is wonderful and exciting to behold the moving of God as He enlarges his territory, but when the music

85

stops and the shouts of praise cease, can we go home and satisfy the sensual needs of the one nearest and dearest to our hearts? Do we have the same desire, zeal or conviction to be consistently intimate with our spouses as we do to win the souls of perfect strangers? Or, has the anointing defected when you desperately needed it in your second most valuable relationship in the world? I'd beg to differ. **Somehow, somewhere we have missed it; we missed the fact that the anointing breaks every single yoke, to include explicitly the yoke of sensual lethargy.** We have most ministries down to a science, we have the right technology and tools for outreach as never before, yet the basic 'tools' we were born with have been left, as it seems, dying prematurely on the vine.

Call it silent and invisible attrition or call it bedroom abandonment, either way we are taking tremendous losses; our casualty toll is outlandishly high and steadily climbing because of our malfunction as a body to take seriously the issues related to righteous sensual intimacy. We have failed miserably while behind closed doors our spouses have suffered in silence for years, you would only be kidding yourself if you think they haven't. They may appear to be thriving on the outside while on the inside they are sensually destitute and silently screaming for sustenance (Ministry) in this area. Sure they will put on a smile in public but they are truly frowning and drowning on the inside.

Husbands your wives see the sincere commitment, time and effort you put into your ministries. Wives, your husband's see the dedication and passion you put into your calling and as you continue to reinvent yourself and thrive in these areas they are screaming 'what about my needs?' 'What about us?' Don't I matter anymore? Why don't we talk anymore? What happened to the hugs? What happened to the kisses? Why don't we hold hands anymore? Why don't you look at me with desire anymore? And, WHY have you stopped making love to me?

You may argue the relevance of such exclamations but the relevance is simply this, we need some HELP! We are proud of your spiritual growth and are in no way threatened by it. Whether it is in the church or in the corporate sector your ministerial progress and ability is exceptional and truly laudable; but believers also require quality time between the sheets. It may surprise you but outside of Christ your primary ministry is not the church, not your friends or associates, it is not your ministerial staff, not your corporate job, and not even your own children!

Your primary ministry is your spouse. God told us to become one with our spouse, not anyone or anything else. Why? Because this oneness represents the ultimate relationship as Christ the Son is with the Father; no other relationship compares to this particular partnership, that's why marriage is so sacred to God.

Your spouse's sexual frustrations are a bona-fide concern and pardon my frankness but you would be a fool to ignore it. It would also be foolish to assume that just because she/he is married to you that they HAVE to tolerate it. Before you dismiss this yearning as worldly or 'being in the flesh' let me ask you this; do you have a zeal for righteousness, holiness and desire more than anything else to please God? Good (I'm *assuming* you said yes), then a similar zeal should be applied to pleasing our spouses and finding industrious ways to keep the sensual drive alive and kicking. This too pleases God.

Side bar: Several years ago a country music artist (Ronnie Milsap, 1983) recorded a hit song "Stranger in My House". The song tells of a man who suspects his wife is fantasizing about being with a secret lover, one of the versus he sang said *"she sits staring out the window a million miles away and when I ask if she's all right she never has too much to say, is it somebody we both know or somebody she just met? Is she loving him in her mind while she's lying here in my bed? There's a stranger in my house, somebody here that I can't see, stranger in my house. There's somebody here trying to take her away from me"*

Is there a stranger in your house?

"Beloved I pray that you may prosper in all things and be in good health, just as your soul prospers" (III John: 2)

Prosperity in ALL THINGS includes your sensual side. Let me be very clear at this juncture: if you are married in Christ, enjoying your God given sexuality and indulging in the pleasantries of sensual fantasy with your spouse is NOT a sin. For the born-again believer who may be offended by this exceptionally candid reading you may be the most in need of the pleasure principles that lie within. I write this with all due respect and in the spirit of love, so please take a moment to consider the fact that intimacy is a ministry and this too is your calling. Just because you got saved and are now a prominent figure in your church doesn't change the natural 'sex factor' in your life but rather affirms it and puts intimacy and our sensuality in perspective. The only thing you need fear is remaining the same and brushing this text off as worldly, perverted and insignificant.

As believers we are excited about the time when we will all get to heaven, as the song says 'what a day of rejoicing that will be'. But even in heaven we will no longer enjoy one of our greatest pleasures, sexual intimacy with our spouse. That's right NO SEX in heaven. Sex is an earthly pleasure we get to indulge in only in this dispensation of time; Jesus said (Mark 12:25) *"in heaven we neither marry nor are given in marriage"*. So, will the Lord say to you concerning the area of your sensual stewardship "well done thou good and faithful servant"? You get to decide that now on this side of heaven.

Couple discussion:

- Can you pinpoint an area in your life that can use some 'modifications' in order for you to give more of yourself to the ministry of intimacy?
- Do you sense that God is calling you into a deeper and richer intimate relationship with your spouse?

- Do you feel intimidated or uncomfortable with the possibility of intimate changes?
- What do you think we can we do as a church to be an example to new disciples in this area?

Prayer:

Our Lord from whom all blessings flow, I praise you with all my heart and soul for the many blessings you have bestowed upon us. You have been our constant provider and you have nurtured us consistently thru the many ministries made available by your spirit. Heavenly Father help us not to falter in serving you in the ministry of our sensuality and I pray that you would convict us daily to safeguard this ministry as we grow in Your precious grace. Keep the 'strangers' out of our bedrooms and help keep us keen to the works of the enemy as he tries to infiltrate our love and affection for each other and strengthen the brethren worldwide for the sustainment of our undefiled intimacy. In the name of Jesus Christ we pray, amen.

Chapter 6

Due Affection
1 Corinthian 7: 1-9

"Let the husband render to his wife the affection due her, and likewise also the wife to her husband."
(1 Corinthians 7:3).

*W*hat do people see when they see you as a couple? Does your non-verbal tones make the statement that your marriage is vibrant and healthy, or does it clearly say that you have been living with a 'roommate' for quite some time? Like it or not your marriage is saying something and somebody, even your children if you are a parent, is watching and learning what you are teaching whether it is good or bad.

We will all leave some kind of legacy behind. Personally, I don't want my professional achievements to overshadow my personal contributions and achievements to my family and friends. I have learned that even in my personal failures there are many lessons to learn and pass on. I've already confessed in my disclaimer that I have been divorced. I can tell you from experience that one of the worst feelings in the world is to go to your own house and be estranged completely from the one you married in order to make your house a home. I didn't know it then, but one of the main problems I had was not talking about it. My machismo got in the way on many occasions and more often than not triggered completely avoidable arguments. I was oblivious to the fact that in order to restore 'it' I needed to talk about 'it'!

So again I ask, what do people see when they see you as a couple? Is love immediately evident or do they have to go searching for 'it' in another couple, on the internet or secular media? Believe it or not, your marriage messages are being read loud and clear by those who know you and strangers alike. As Christians, there's another issue we need to be concerned about and that is what Christ looks like on us as we wear Him in our marriages.

At first glance, the first few verses in this scripture (1 Cor. 7) describe a mind boggling concept; a concept that is seemingly foreign to most western civilizations. The idea that a person's body not belonging to them but to another as it pertains to sexual intimacy sounds unfathomable, outdated and subservient. Yet here, we see it in black and white in what is arguably the holiest book in the world. So why should the author of this text even have to go there and make such a suggestion (not a command)? What was going on, even at the time of these writing, that would make the highly respected apostle Paul say that it's better to marry than to burn (in hell, with lust, or illicit passion) if two people can't refrain from sexual immorality (fornication)? You guessed it—the same thing that was going on then is the same thing that's going on now, it was sex on steroids, defiled intimacy run amuck!

Let me be clear, I do not suggest extolling your spouse with the first few verses of this text, it will definitely thwart any and all momentum you may have had in set-ting the mood. However, I do suggest that we consider the underlying premise here that as a married couple we have dedicated our bodies not only to Christ but to our spouses as well, specifically for the sake of sensual intimacy. Not forcibly, not through coercion or intimida-tion but voluntarily and lovingly. I tend to believe that if we can come to grips with this particular concept of submission and humility in a godly and loving way, we would then experience more fulfilling marital relation-ships and our intimacy would soar.

"Nevertheless, because of sexual immorality, let each man have his own wife, and let each woman have her own husband"
(I Corinthians 7:2).

Does this text insinuate or imply OWNERSHIP? Absolutely! However, this is not referring to the kind of ownership that would turn your spouse into some kind of a second class servant or slave; but rather a mutu-ally beneficial partnership of sorts. In essence— Paul is saying that there should not be a 'need' for you to look any further than your spouse to fulfill your intimate requirements. Note in verse 4 where the apostle Paul extols us by saying that the wife does not have authority over her own body, but the husband does. And likewise the husband does not have authority over his own body, but the wife does.

Paul is driving a crucial point home here. He is referring to what should be our willingness to give ourselves completely to our partners. Before going any further, I suppose some would ask; why should the church take the lead and be more open in its discussions and direction about sensual matters? Or, why should the church fast and pray for the intimate healing of our bedrooms? Why should the church even care if married Christian couples are sensually impoverished or not? So long as we put on a happy face and continue to serve the body of Christ in other areas right?

Well, the church should care and be concerned because to love and be loved is one of our deepest desires, greatest needs and most admittedly one of our most dominating daily thoughts. We were created with these desires and needs and our significant other completes this quest for fulfillment. It's also a deal-breaker outside of the marriage covenant and the only instance in scripture where Christ Himself says explicitly that divorce can be—but doesn't have to be—an option for remedy. Sexcapades (fornication, adultery) outside of the marriage covenant can have devastating consequences, to say the least. Not only is it sin against God but the bible declares that whoever commits sexual immorality sins against their own body (I Cor 6:18).

So I ask again, why should the church even consider talking about Christianity between the sheets with a tad bit more fervor? For the sake of curiosity let's take a gander at some statistical info on divorce and some of the reasons for divorce.

Here are some often cited reasons given for deciding to divorce:

- The couple falls 'out' of love/the relationship runs out of steam
- Communication breakdown
- Infidelity
- Loss of interest
- Marrying too young
- Emotional or physical abuse
- Lack of commitment
- Too much arguing
- Unrealistic expectations
- Lack of equality in the relationship

Here are some other stats:

- In 2000 58 million couples were married, yet separated.
- In 2000 there were over 21 million divorces.
- People between the ages of 25 to 39 make up 60% of all divorces.
- Over one million children are affected by divorce each year.
- Approximately 1/3 of divorced parents remain bitter and hostile several years after the divorce.
- More people are part of second marriages today than first marriages.
- One-quarter of all Americans have experienced at least one divorce.

The top six signs of an impending divorce include:

1) Dreaming of life without the spouse
2) The bad in the marriage outweighs the good
3) Lack of communication
4) Engaging in negative defense mechanisms such as sarcasm or being dismissive
5) Loneliness, feelings of depression and hopelessness
6) The couple rarely, if ever, has sex

Divorce statistics are generally calculated by comparing the number of divorces with the number of marriages in a given time period.

No matter how imprecise some of this data may be, we would be quite negligent if we ignored the reality of these factors seeing that many 'Christians', myself included, have found themselves among the long list of victims. Nevertheless, this small sampling of data does not make our marital calling any less urgent but rather intensifies our responsibility. These stats break Gods heart and should speak volumes to believers. We can reverse this trend but it would take an unprecedented and monumental paradigm shift that would revive of our hearts and our priorities.

I am the product of a 'broken home' so I know what it's like to be raised by a single mother and be left alone to figure out life (and sex) in isolation. We need to stop living in fear of straight sex discussions and embrace the fact that sex was Gods idea in the first place and He put it in the context of marriage for a reason.

Our embrace, our touch, our desire etc. is due our spouse and theirs is to us. Outside of Christ our marriages are the most profound and impactful relationships in our lives—so let's demystify our sensuality and rid ourselves of senseless stigmas that cause us to be ashamed of our intimacy.

Life as God intended puts our intimacy into perspective and properly obeyed would produce pure and untainted results. We must admit that the world and its rebellious anti-Christ ways is reaping what it has sown and these faulty relationships have crept ever so slightly into the pulpits and pews known as the Church of the Living God. The spread of disease caused by sexual sins cannot be disputed no matter what belief system you claim. These plagues are indiscriminate (sins against the body) and boast names like AIDS, gonorrhea, syphilis, herpes, clap and the like. Go figure, God knew and knows what He was talking about when he commanded us to abstain from fornication and adultery. God designed sex to be monogamous and within the borders of a marriage covenant, a holy and committed union.

If you and your spouse were virgins when you got married then praise the Lord! I would like to meet you if only just to stare at you in AWE ☺ it's an amazing feat in this day and age but NOT an impossible feat. I believe we can raise Godly children and teach them to respect one other as they obey God and WAIT for marriage before becoming sexually active. Can I get an AMEN?

Ok, so if you are like me then you definitely were not a virgin when you got married and had more than a handful of partners prior to 'settling down'. Don't worry about how many so-called lovers you had because once you are Born-again not even God keeps count (Whew! thank goodness). As it pertains to adultery, you are still not alone. I failed in this are as well in my previous marriage. Oh by the way, marriage as an institution is perfect and never fails, it is the people who fail their marriages, but that's another study for another time. Anyway, I have since repented of my failure although it ended in divorce. I can personally attest that fornication and adultery are not the way to go and here's one of the many reasons why. Whether we like it or not or believe it or not, a person who has had multiple sexual partners is left with the residue or 'impressions' of each lover they have been with. Some evangelicals have titled these impressions as 'soul ties'.

These impressions apparently spill over into every other sexual relationship thereafter and may cause competing sensual images that can ruin your current relationship with your spouse. For example: the sensual chemistry between you and one of your previous sexual partners may have been phenomenal. In bed their unmatched energy and arousal caused you to have a myriad of orgasms, the likes of which you have never experienced. Consequently, for one reason or another, that relationship came to an end and your present partner, which may have ended up being your spouse, barely stimulates you. Guess who you think about when the idea of having sex is brought up? You honestly think about that previous partner and how awesome the sensual chemistry was, right? There is an intangible and undeniable connection between sex and the soul. You can't give your body without it affecting your inner being (soul). Again, this is why the bible tells us that he that is sexually immoral sins against their very own body.

Now multiply that example by 5, 10, 20 or more sexual partners in a lifetime. No wonder why we have such a skewed and disturbing perception of the purpose of sex in the church. Sexcapades, as I call it, have lifetime consequences, very much like the smoker who finally quits smoking but whose health is still deteriating and ultimately dies of lung cancer.

Although we are forgiven by God and he can and does heal us emotionally, many couples have to live with the residue resulting from the sexually un-pure choices that were made in the body until the Day comes when we trade in this earthly body for a heavenly one. Until then, by God's grace and forgiveness let's proceed with making the best of what we have left knowing that with God's help, and the unconditional love and support of our spouses we can be to our mate everything they want and need between the sheets. We can 'duly' give our bodies to each other knowing we are in good hands.

Couple discussion:

- How would you define the concept of body 'Ownership' as described by Paul?
- What are some of your thoughts on the statistics mentioned?
- Do you believe the church should have the lead role in the sexual revolution of Christian couples? If no, why not?
- What are your thoughts on sensual 'soul ties'?

Prayer:

Heavenly Father, we welcome you each and every day into the bedroom of our minds. Help us to be considerate of our spouses needs and to make their fulfillment a priority in our lives. Despite the many other obligations we have in our lives let us never forget the one you called us to become one with. My prayer is that Christians all over the world will with love, prayer and purpose provide the due affection to our mates that you designed for us to have. Let your Holy Spirit continue to lead us and teach us, this we pray in Jesus name. Amen.

Chapter 7

The Big '3' of the Bedroom

—⚊—

"Nevertheless let every one of you (husbands) in particular so love his wife even as himself; and the wife see that she respect her husband."

(Ephesians 5:33)

D r. E. Emerson put together an incredible book titled:: Love and Respect. It's the right book for the right time and I'd highly recommend adding it to your library. Summarily, his book expounds in great detail on Ephesians chapter 5. From verse 33 specifically, we extrapolate that the wife thrives on his love toward her as the husband thrives on her respect toward him and in the absence of love and respect belies the marital chaos that we see all too often today.

In order for spouses to truly become intimate with each other we must understand that not only do we define intimacy differently but we express that desire differently as well. Someone jokingly stated that, men are like microwaves and women are like crock pots when it comes to sexual performance, but that would be for each couple to gauge and judge. Nonetheless, I don't consider such a quip very comical. Generally speaking of course men are basic and simple creatures. We are visually stimulated and it doesn't take a whole lot to get us interested or excited. But don't get it twisted; we like to be romanced and to romance as well. Women, on the other hand, are not so unassuming. This wonderful creature can be very complicated and challenging to entice and satisfy. That's just the way God wired us, as Dr. Emerson would say "not weird just different". There isn't a magic potion or a magical mantra that can be spoken over your spouse to turn them into the erogenous damsel or Romeo you want them to be. Just understand that we both want the same thing but we require or NEED to take different routes to get there. I refer to our joint needs as *the **Big Three of the Bedroom***:

1. Emotional connection (or chemistry)
2. Stimulation
3. Mutual satisfaction

As we briefly expound on the big 3 the real question that will need to be answered is this. Are you willing to do whatever it takes to understand that it is ok to have sensual differences between you and your spouse and not become frustrated with the process of uniting them for a continued gratifying sensual experience?

"What a happy and holy fashion it is that those who love one another should rest on the same pillow"
– Nathaniel Hawthorne

Ok, so let's break it down.

Emotional connection- Where would we be without chemistry? Not very far. One of the main ingredients for successful sports teams, businesses and marriage is chemistry. The ability to click and gel together toward a common cause is a beautiful and rewarding thing. Without it failure would soon rear its head in victory. Have you ever been in relationships where everything is such a strain and the stress in the atmosphere is palpable? Most relationships like that eventually come to a crashing halt. Fortunately, it is possible to avert the disaster of a failed relationship so long as someone is willing to admit that they need to make a drastic change. Our level of emotional connectivity with our spouse is entirely in our hands, every moment of every day. Never forget, we are the ones in charge of and responsible for our moods and emotions. We can blame a lot of stuff on others, and we do, but we are ultimately responsible for how we feel emotionally and how we respond emotionally. Let's take a cue on emotional restraint from Jesus Himself, straight out of John chapter eight verses 3-11.

This is one of my favorite passages in the bible, it's the story of a woman caught in the very act of adultery. The religious leaders of the day (scribes and Pharisees) snatched her out of the bed {apparently it was ok for men to be caught because whatever happened to the man involved remains a mystery} at any rate they dragged her to where Jesus was and tossed her mercilessly at His feet. I imagine the emotionally charged atmosphere as people slowly began gathering to see what was going on. Then came the accusation of adultery and the immediate judgment and punishment (stoning) that must follow according to the Law of Moses. Little did they know that Jesus was above the Law (so to speak).

He ignored their attempts to try and stir His emotions against her. By now this charged atmosphere was stirring the crowd and perhaps some were even scurrying the grounds for a sizable stone to pitch her way once the sentence was passed, but not Jesus.

He remained calm and cool while bending down to scribble a thing or two in the dirt. I'd love to read whatever it was He wrote. Finally, with great relief from the crowd, He spoke these timely, potent and awe inspiring words *"He who is without sin among you, let him throw a stone at her first"* and then He stooped back down to write on the ground. You know the story; one by one they dropped their stones and went away taking their emotionally charged atmosphere with them. Jesus remained in control of His emotions and saw above and beyond the accusations, He told the woman if no one else condemns you then neither do I *"go and sin no more"*. What a relief it must have been for her to know that she was in the wrong, deserved to die, was at the brink of being stoned to death and found pardon from the new Man in town.

Oh, God help us get control of our emotions like Jesus demonstrated in this story! What if you immediately forgave your spouse for an offense? What if we chose to comfort instead of condemn? What if we chose to compliment instead of criticize? What if _____ (you fill in the blank). We could have a lot less arguments if we had more control of our emotions and embrace the chemistry we share. We could love each other better if we could just get control of our emotions. We could have better intimacy and perhaps even cuddle more often, if we could just get control of our emotions. We can choose to get along if we want to. Husbands and wives can be the best of friends if they choose to be, taking it one day at a time. I urge you not to let the storms in your marriage control the tempo of your bedroom; choose to calm the storm, speak to the tumultuous winds and say 'peace be still'.

I cannot leave John: 8 alone until I share with you what I really admire about this text—and what was a true revelation to me. The fact of the matter was that Jesus was the only legitimate person standing there without sin and could have justifiably bricked the woman to death but He chose the route of passion and forgiveness instead. He carefully crafted His response to the adulteresses' accusers by saying *"he who is without sin AMONG YOU. . . (Emphasis mine)"* Jesus was not 'among' or a part of their group! Had he been "among them' He would have no choice but to obey His own command. Remember, He was the only person there without sin; very cool huh and quite a clever response.

So, what do you choose when your spouse gets on your last nerve? I pray that you too will choose the path of passion; the results are much more favorable.

Stimulation- Sensual stimulation means stimulation that involves all of the senses, especially that of touch. Sensual spots exist all over the bodies of both men and women and we would do well exploring what excites our spouses to the heights of true ecstasy. This exploration may include the likes of a sensual massage, tender caresses or even erotic fantasy chatter. You may also want to consider trying different and more arousing sexual positions; this can be a wonderful time for you and your spouse to bring newness to the bedroom. Your imagination is your only limitation.

Mutual satisfaction- I think it's safe to state that men are most guilty of the offense of being selfish lovers. Ephesians 5: 28-29 tells us that ". . .*husbands should love their own wives as their own bodies; he who loves his wife loves himself. For no one ever hated his own flesh, but NOURISHES and CHERISHES it, just as the lord does the church*". **It's not all about you fellas. We**

have to do a better job of listening and learning about her needs. More pointedly, just because you had an orgasm and are completely satisfied and ready to chill doesn't mean that your wife did and believe me she is NOT ready to chill. If maintaining stamina is an issue I would highly recommend speaking with a doctor or sex therapist and getting the help and treatment you need. There's nothing to be embarrassed about gents, Viagra, and drugs like it, are extremely potent and popular for a reason. The letter to the Ephesians by the hands of Paul is very clear on not only nourishing and cherishing our own bodies but likewise we are to ensure that our spouses are mutually benefiting from this intricate and exclusive care.

I don't claim to assume that everyone will agree with the big 3 as I have stated them, these are clearly not all inclusive. There are myriad books and research on marital intimacy by renowned sex therapist and professionals for you to choose from. You may want to continue to gather information in order to make the best decision for you and your partner. I only ask that you do something, whatever it takes, to make and keep intimacy a priority.

Couple discussion

- Can you identify when there is sexual tension in your home?
- Do you feel as if your needs are more important or greater than your spouse's needs? If so, why?
- Have you both discussed what your needs are? If not, why not?
- Have you really taken the time to discuss the big 3?
- What can you both do to have a better understanding of each other's God given sensual needs?
- If there is a sexual dysfunction or medical condition have you sought help?
- If needed, would you consider sex therapy or marriage counseling to get your sex life on track?

Prayer

Blessed Lord and King, may we ever be mindful of the special and intricate needs of each other. Help us not be falter in the pursuit of lasting emotional connections, stimulations and mutual satisfaction in our intimacy. We thank you for al you've done in our hearts thus far and we thank you for what You will continue to do. In Jesus name we pray.

Amen

Chapter 8

Public Displays of Affection (PDA's)

—◠◡◠—

"It's not enough that your partner knows that you take pride in his or her accomplishments. You have to show it. Making a fuss over the small, good things that happen every day can boost the health of your marriage."
(T. Parker-Pope, 2010)

*I*f you haven't already figured it out, it's the little things that make such a big difference and mean so much to our significant other. If you want to keep the embers of passion burning simply put another log on the fire. If you are out of wood then find something else that will feed the flame. These are the logs of 'affection due' husband and wife that are specifically set aside for our indulgences. I am surprised at the number of married Christian couples that I have met in public that don't even hold hands or hug each other. It's as if they are with a total stranger or at the very least a distant acquaintance.

This unnatural estrangement was not intended; that person walking next to you is not your 5th cousin, it's your spouse! Render unto her the affection due her! Love is a verb, an ACTION word. You gotta do something. We do not and cannot love in word only but we must love in deed as well (See 1 John 3:18) that means that our love toward each other requires deliberate action, something visual that has to be seen and physically felt. We have a living, breathing, functioning and tangible kind of love. Jesus told His disciples (John 14:15) *"if you love me keep my commandments"*, keeping His commandments requires effort on our part so we cannot love passively. Our love for and toward our spouses should be robust and evident even outside the secret confines of the physical bedroom.

In the Garden of Eden, Adam and Eve basked in a sinless environment "and they were both naked, the man and his wife, and were not ashamed" (Gen 2:25). After the fall, the environment became contaminated and sin entered the world. At once they realized they were naked and shamefully covered themselves; God asked them a question that was never answered. God asked "who told you that you were naked?" We have no record of them being told this by anyone, as far as we can tell sin simply brought shame to their conscious- ness and made them cover themselves.

Thousands of years later a Savior would arrive to become our sacrifice for the fall of man and remove this curse of sin forever. To wit, we can be naked again, a man and his wife, and not be ashamed. I am not advo- cating public nudity or indecent public behavior; I am advocating not being ashamed to show your love for your spouse publicly when they are fully clothed. These forms of intimacy (PDA's) are an extension of your bed- room behavior.

Hear (read) this carefully: There is an unspoken (positive) statement that is made when people come in contact with Christian couples who intentionally and audaciously show their love for one another. It is a strong witness for the world to see a born again husband and wife holding hands, embracing, or even light kissing in public. They are naked, transparent in their feelings for each other and they are not ashamed.

In the 26th chapter of the book of Genesis, Abimelech, king of the Philistines, said to Isaac *"quite OBVIOUSLY she is YOUR WIFE"* (Emphasis mine), when he SAW Isaac show endearment (PDA's) to Rebekah his wife. There was something about the way in which Isaac caressed Rebekah that sent the message that this woman is mine. This message was profound and unmistakable and clearly says this person has been given to me by the Lord and I love them without hesitation or the intimidation of others. Never let the world dictate your actions and responses to your spouse. Your PDA's will make even a king repent and bless you!

The holding of that hand sends the message to your spouse that you cherish them, that hug means I care about you immensely, and that kiss says you mean the world to me! Your spouse won't be worried about you checking out some other guy or gal when they have your undivided attention in these areas. If you can only be intimate in private I would wonder what you were trying to hide in public. Are you embarrassed to be with the man or woman you chose as your spouse?

"The more closely we see ourselves being watched by our enemies (unbelievers) the more intent we should be to avoid their slanders so that their ill-will strengthens

us in the desire to do well. Therefore, as believers, we should strive to be exemplary in every aspect of our lives; doing our best for the sake of Christ and His gospel. . .unbelievers will be attracted to the gospel that they see in the life of the believer"

(J. Bridges, 2006)

Some of you may argue that PDA's can be faked; you may also argue that PDA's don't necessarily mean your spouse really loves you and that your relationship is on cloud nine. I caution you again, this book is for born again believers who have had a real born again experience. Like the steps of a righteous man, our affection toward each other is literally ordered by the Lord. If our relationships are not on cloud nine or seem to be less than ideal, then we should be taking every measure to ensure we head in the direction of reviving our level of intimacy. That's the purpose of this book. Funny (not really) how we can make all the excuses in the world when it comes to being intimate, what are you afraid of? Take it in faith and you will find that PDA's are rightfully yours to indulge. I guarantee you that your spouse will thank and appreciate you for it.

Christians need to take PDA's back from the world. Why is it that the world readily displays their misappropriated affection without any reservations and the body of Christ gets offended or appalled by the sight of believers showing their desire toward each other in public? This is so backwards! We are the true witnesses to the world in what romance is all about NOT the other way around. Let's put the honor of PDA's back in marriages as God grants us the time in this dispensation.

"Husbands love your wives, just as Christ also loved the church and gave Himself for her"
(Ephesians 5:25)

Admittedly, brothers have struggled in the PDA arena, but as leaders and priests of our homes we must overcome false stereotypes of thinking that we will lose cool points or thinking that PDA's are for 'Sissy's' or 'girlie men. On the contrary, your manhood is on display; it's the strength and understanding of your marital office on display. When someone else is checking out your spouse, you don't have to get angry or intimidated; take it as a compliment that you have great taste but at the same time this admirer needs to know (by your PDA's) that your spouse is covered by your affection and that your lover is not up for grabs.

On the flip side, the lack of your PDA's could send the message that you're not serious about each other; you are both available and are looking for love in all the wrong places. Sounds like the perfect set of circumstances for the enemy to set-up shop and wreak havoc in your marriage doesn't it? So, if you don't show an interest (in public) in your spouse beware lest another does. The choice is entirely up to you.

"Wisdom is the principal thing;
therefore get wisdom. . ."
(Proverbs 4: 7)

Another area we can improve in is the way we sometimes allow a television show or a sporting event to hamper moments of intimacy. You may shout all over the house when your team scores a touchdown but you're as quiet as a mouse when it comes to expressing your intimate side to your spouse. What gives? How can we (I'm guilty too) pay so much attention to sports, reality shows, etc.; remember every player in every game yet fail to remember our own wedding anniversary or our spouses' birthday? Shame on us! As fascinating and innovative our society has become we have to admit that TV is a poor aphrodisiac. Why do we get caught up in the drama of General Hospital, All My Children and the Young and the Restless as the Days of our Lives continue to deteriorate? These shows may influence your interaction with your spouse (in negative ways) more than you care to fess up to.

Your real life marriage is not a TV program and there are no directors to yell "cut" when things go awry between you and your loved one. There are no scripted lines prepared well in advance to cause you to fall into the arms of your lover and live happily ever after. This is real life and our marriages take real work, real commitment, and real intimacy. Where are the shows that promote godly living and godly marriages? Where are the shows that promote the undefiled bedroom and give God glory for our spouses? The only godly show or representation the world is going to see is in our PDA's. Our affection is on display for the world to see God's pure love in marriage. Don't be a slave to your television and please don't let all your waking hours be spent being intimate with an inanimate object that can never return your affection.

I'm not against TV or being a sports fan. I enjoy a good show or a game just as much as the next person but whatever the sport or show that you indulge in with such fanaticism should not get in the way of your affection and steal PDA's from your spouse. Those we see and admire on the big screen won't be found in our bedroom and they couldn't care less about our marital or sensual fulfillment. Additionally, we need to be careful who we idolize because many athletes and movie stars live quite contrary to the Holy Scriptures and don't have the slightest interest in anything outside of their own comfort, wealth, and fame. We have encountered men and women who claim Christianity yet are completely controlled by video games, sports, and TV programs. This is an addiction that needs to be repented of, not that its sinful but because it exceeds moderation and should not be allowed to control the climate of our homes, our attitudes and especially not the climate of our bedrooms. I challenge you to do a sincere PDA background check and you may find that the big screen has been the culprit in the demise of your acts of intimacy toward your mate.

Also, if you and your spouse argue all the time and you both have 'strong willed' (stubborn) personalities, then someone needs to be mature and humbled enough (Men) to take a stand against this demonic stronghold. Identify this intruder as the thief breaking into your home to ravish and destroy you, whip him unapologetically with the word of God, and banish him from your bedroom (professional Christian counseling may help also). We must be active participants in our marriages and throw a wrench in the enemy's devious plans by being the first to apologize and the first to make amends. Relentlessly pursue the forgiveness of your spouse with the utmost sincerity and then get your sex back! It is THE CHURCH that needs to bring sexy back NOT Justin Timberlake!

Remember the sage advice of King Solomon that *"a soft answer turns away wrath"* (Proverbs 15:1). So, don't keep picking at the problem by constantly bringing up each other's past mistakes and stabbing each other with harsh words. This will only lead to further trauma in your relationship and stunt the growth of your intimacy. Stop the hemorrhaging now and let the Great Physician heal you. *"Do not let the sun go down on your wrath"* (Ephesians 4:26) doesn't mean that all disputes will be resolved within 24hrs, but it does mean that we should refuse to allow disputes to fester and have dominion over our relationships. We need to do our best to refuse to allow differences of opinion to contaminate brand new days of grace and mercy.

If God Himself has forgiven our spouses of their past sins then who are we to bring up what God has discarded as far as the east is from the west? We are fully cognizant that there are times when disagreements take many days to be settled and PDA's are the last thing on your mind, but these should be the exception not the rule. C.S Lewis said it best "to be a Christian is to forgive the inexcusable because God has forgiven the inexcusable you".

I do not blithely suggest that healing is in your hands but I wish I could shout it from the hills and mountaintops of the world that 'Healing is in your hands'! Your touch matters, your embrace is full of medicinal wonders, our touch was meant to heal not to hurt. On the particular occasions that PDA's are in jeopardy reconciliation should take immediate priority. II Corinthians 5:19 tells us that we have been given the ministry of reconciliation and although friction is inevitable in our relationships with the proper tools and intentional practice it can be kept to a minimum while our love lives thrive with robust euphoric energy.

Be cognizant that the smallest form of the church is where two (you and your spouse) are gathered together in His name. This is the ultimate dynamic duo! The sooner your relationship gets out of the 'red' the more profitable the kingdom will be and we all benefit. Remember your witness; God wants a return on His invested gift (marriage) to us. Our PDA's are shown in some very simple ways that we may not even be aware of. For example: a romantic dinner for just the two of you or taking a stroll together in the park. How about dance lessons or self-defense classes together? Get the idea?

Anything you and your spouse do together in public (and private) should be done with love and affection on display. That's how the world is going to see God manifest in the flesh. This is marriage 101 no PhD's required, just PDA's.

Another note to my brothers: This is in no way a conclusive list but PDA's are shown when you walk closest to the curb when you are both walking down the street. Where I grew up if you walked down the street with your lady on the curb side it meant that she was unprotected and available. This was one way the neighborhood pimps would guide his prostitutes down the street and they would await the honk of a horn that meant someone was looking to pay for a treat. By you (the male) walking on the curb side meant that you were her protector and she was not available, no horns. This was street etiquette and it has stayed with me through the years. I've explained this to my wife when we first met and she really appreciates the gesture even if it is folklore.

PDA's include opening her car door and making sure she's buckled in before you drive off. It includes walking beside or slightly behind her on the way up a flight of stairs and beside or slightly in front of her on the way down. It includes pulling out her seat for her and allowing her to order her food before you order yours and saying grace together before you eat. I truly believe that God smiles on these acts of chivalry and the benefits are mutually beneficial. I must also interject that PDA's include praising and complimenting each other. Verbally trashing your spouse in private or public is irresponsible, immature and has the potential to hinder your prayers (men). See 1 Peter 3:7. God unequivocally frowns on this type of unproductive dialog. Cast it out of your lives immediately, its robbing you and your spouse of invaluable experiences.

Once you get a true revelation of the mutual benefits of PDA's your entire relationship with your spouse will soar to exhilarating new heights. Some say it's all about the Benjamin's but as it pertains to PDA's it's all about the dividends my brothers and sisters, God bless those dividends.

With my emphasis added lets read King Solomon's 'The Virtuous Wife' as described in <u>Proverbs 31: 10-31</u>:

". . .*who can find a virtuous wife? For her worth is far above rubies. The heart of her husband safely trusts her; so he will have no lack of gain. She does him GOOD and not evil al the days of her life. She seeks wool and flax, and willingly works with her hands. She is like the merchant ships; she brings her food from afar. She also rises while it is yet night, and provides food for her household and a portion for her maidservants. (Old Testament Business Woman) She considers a field and buys it (an independent woman); from her profits she plants a vineyard. She girds herself with strength, and strengthens her arms (she must work out☺).*

She perceives that her merchandise is good and her lamp does not go out all night. (WOW step aside Lionel Ritchie this is what 'All night long' is all about). . . .she stretches her hands to the distaff and her hand holds the spindle. She extends her hands to the poor, yes; she reaches out her hands to the needy (missionary minded woman). She is not afraid of snow for her household for her household is clothed with scarlet. She makes tapestry for herself; her clothing is fine linen and purple. Her husband is known in the gates, when he sits among the elders of the land. She makes linen garments and sells them, and supplies sashes for the merchants. Strength and honor are her clothing; she shall rejoice in time to come. She opens her mouth with wisdom and on her tongue is the law of kindness (not sarcasm). She watches over the ways of her household and does not eat the bread of her idleness. Her children rise up and call her blessed; **her husband also,** *and* **he praises her.** *Many daughters have done well, but you excel them all. Charm is deceitful and beauty is passing, but a woman who fears the Lord,* **she shall be praised.** *Give her of the fruit of her hands, and let her own woks praise her in the gates" (Emphasis mine).*

Husbands praise your wives during the day and she will praise you at night. And the church said 'Amen'.

<u>Couple discussion:</u>
- What do your PDA's look like now?
- What do you want your PDA's to look like tomorrow?
- What do YOU need to do to get your PDA's back?
- Are you ashamed of yourself or your spouse?
- How can you prove to be more affectionate to your spouse?

- To get an objective opinion, would you consider asking a close and trusted associate how they see your relationship?

Prayer:

Dear Lord, thank you once again for such a wonderful opportunity to show our love to our spouses in ways that will communicate genuine affection and care. Help us as we become one, to not get in the way of our own progress by allowing selfishness to get the glory instead of selflessness. Grant us the grace to be consistent in praising our spouses and filling their ears with affirmation. We believe you are the center of our relationship and desire our intimacy to draw us closer to you as we draw closer to each other. We now know that our love is on display in public; as your witnesses help us make a heartfelt and genuine effort to represent marital PDA's in an attractive and positive way. This we pray in Jesus name amen.

Chapter 9

Mom & Pop
(The Kid Factor)

—ᴡ—

"Many parents don't realize the gift they give their
children by allowing themselves to be seen as a loving

couple. . .if children see that you're comfortable with your sexuality, that's a good model for them"

(J. Berman & L. Berman, 2001)

*D*isputes and disagreements in a relationship are inevitable and finding time can become quite challenging as we juggle work and domestic duties. But God hardwired us for intimacy and created marriage to be good for us. We may not be swinging from the chandeliers every night but it is imperative that we make the effort on a regular basis to have intimate moments however subtle.

Being intimate with your mate is a lifetime endeavor. However, as we go through the stages of this thing called life our mind and bodies naturally change as well. We know that naturally and scientifically, both men and women experience decreased hormone levels of estrogen and testosterone. Apparently, men more so experience reduced levels of testosterone; a hormone made by your body and is responsible for the normal growth and development of the male sex organs and for maintenance of other sexual characteristics. Women experience diminutions in the hormone estrogen. Estrogen (the primary female sex hormone) is the general name for a group of hormone compounds. It is the main sex hormone in women and is critical to the menstrual cycle. Although both men and women have this hormone, it is found in higher amounts in women, especially those capable of reproducing.

We have already established that intimacy is far more than just sex; yet making time, to be intimate or to have sex, as parents will need to include a shifting of your day to day responsibilities. For example, you may want to try sharing the chores in the house or taking turns cooking, this will help break up the monotony a bit and may even be seen as a loving and welcome gesture by your spouse. Consider these suggestions as you make way for intimacy:

- Establishing a date night
- Take one another to a couples massage
- Create a new way to court each other
- Write each other a love letter and mail it
- Spend a little extra time touching each other
- Be tender and kind in your conversation
- Listen more, talk less
- Spend more time in foreplay
- Watch a good romantic comedy together
- Make each other FEEL loved
- Be more selfless instead of selfish

To some, any of these suggestions would require a gargantuan effort and a huge sacrifice of humility; but I've heard it said that humility is not thinking less of oneself but rather thinking of oneself less. Oh by the way, Jesus Christ was the epitome of humility; He humbled himself and became obedient to death on the cross. Intimacy and sex are indispensable ingredients in our marriages. Being patient and trying to understand your mate instead of getting frustrated by them will help resolve conflicts surrounding intimacy.

You may have been excited about each other early on in the relationship but the novelty began to fade. Scientific evidence suggests that the brain chemical 'dopamine' is very high early on in a relationship and declines the longer we stay together. What's interesting about this is that couples that have remarried in their 40's and 50's have the same dopamine levels and feelings of euphoria and hapless romance as those in their early 20's. So I'm praying for our dopamine levels to stay high well into our golden years. We can still arouse each other if we make the effort to do so. If you think it's a stretch just ask Abraham and Sarah.

"And the Lord visited Sarah as He had said, and the Lord did for Sarah as He had spoken. For Sarah

conceived and bore Abraham a son in his old age, at the set time of which God had spoken to him. And Abraham called the name of his son who was born to him—whom Sarah bore to him—Isaac. Then Abraham circumcised his son Isaac when he was eight days old, as God had commanded him. Now Abraham was one hundred years old when his son Isaac was born to him. And Sarah said, "God has made me laugh, and all who hear will laugh with me." She also said, "Who would have said to Abraham that Sarah would nurse children? For I have borne him a son in his old age."

(Genesis 21: 1-7)

Our God is no respecter of persons, what he did for Abraham & Sarah he can do for you too. That's why it's incumbent on us to seek new and creative ways to love one another. It may sound naïve to you but I am acutely aware that sometimes we will experience a lull in our sex drives but let that be the exception and not the rule.

Remember, our relationships are not based on the physical changes we will experience as we age but rather on our continued love, respect and commitment to each other. Sex is just one form of intimacy so in the event that sex is something that you can no longer participate in that doesn't mean that intimacy ends.

When or children were born our relationship went from being exclusively the two of us to a triage and then some. I needed to be patient and gentle as my wife's body adjusted to the physical traumas associated with child bearing and delivery. It can take several months for a woman's body to regain some semblance of normalcy and oftentimes sex is definitely not a priority. Infants are joyfully exhausting and they can run roughshod over a marriage and intimacy.

As parents we unequivocally love our children and are obligated and privileged to raise them in the fear and admonition of the Lord. We make incredible sacrifices for our children that they are often clueless about and never fully appreciate until they themselves become parents. Unfortunately, many times it seems like more and more children are raising their parents instead of the other way around. We have encountered children who intimidate and control their parents and the tempo of the home; in the process the marriage crumbles under the pressure and the initial intimacy that ultimately resulted in the conception of children are now in jeopardy.

On October 13th 1990 my son was born. I was overcome with an unexplainable joy. I remember looking at his adorable little face as if he were the most important person in the world; I was 21 yrs old at the time and had seen dozens of babies up to that point but the child I was holding so tenderly in my arms was MINE! This was MY son and it was a proud moment that I will never forget. My beautiful daughter came along 2 yrs. later and she too has brought a joy to the soul that only 'one's OWN child' can bring. I love them both very dearly but intimacy definitely took a back seat during those early years; we were so consumed with caring for them that we forgot (or was too exhausted) to care for ourselves. We failed to realize that one day our darling little children would grow up and would no longer need (or require) us to spend our every waking moment waiting on them.

Let's face it, having children changes EVERYTHING and forces us to make some serious vicissitudes to our daily lives albeit the command to become with our spouse doesn't change one iota. Parents, I feel your pain and your pleasure of parenting. Kids can put a burdensome hamper on intimacy with your mate and leave you wondering where do we go from here? How do we find the time, the energy, and the will to remain obedient? If you have not already, soon you will notice that as long as you keep feeding and nourishing your children, they will grow before your very eyes and you will wonder where all the time went. Next thing you know years have passed and the 'kids' are now young adults and they begin to carve out their own path in life. We expense our time, resources, and attention to their every whim; we exhaust ourselves for years trying to keep them productive until they grow up. We love them and pray to God that our efforts were not in vain as thy finally leave the nest.

Afterward, you're at home with this total stranger you once knew as your soul mate. You spent the last 18 yrs or so catering to the needs of your offspring and somehow estranged your mate in the process. More likely than not, your body has been transformed from an hour glass shape to a frumpy lump of leftovers. The hair has grayed and thinned, the abdomen area is a bit wider and your former six pack is surprisingly down to one. Your desires have changed, perhaps your goals and dreams diminished and your plans for a second honeymoon look more like plans to separate. Who is this stranger in our homes anyway and where has our love, lust and intimacy gone? Sadly, this happens more often than any of us care to admit. In the name of being a 'good parent' wife you've lost your husband; in the name of raising your kids' husband you've lost your wife. It could happen to any of us, no one is immune but it doesn't have to end this way. There is HOPE!

This is not a cheap shot or a negative blow to our children; kids unwittingly do what kids do but this book is about reviving intimacy in our marriages regardless of whether we have children or not. For the most part kids are very selfish; all they think about is themselves and their wants, their desires, their needs. As loving and responsible parents we want our children to have the best, we want them to be better than we were, we want them to choose to follow Christ and be happy. We want them to love and respect others. We want them educated and to learn good values and behave ethically. Yes! We want them to have exceptional moral principles, character and integrity and we want them to become positive contributors to society; but not at the cost of our marriages, not at the cost of the wife you adore and not at the cost of the husband you pledged your allegiance to and last but not least, NOT at the cost of our intimacy!

If we raise our children to honor God, do good and be responsible citizens and then lose our own marriage in the process then we are hypocrites. If we teach our children to love and respect others and lose our marriages in the process then we are hypocrites. If we teach our children to cherish relationships and that blood is thicker than water and then lose our second most valuable relationship in the world then we are hypocrites. If we have succeeded in raising our children and losing our marriages then we are hypocrites. Being a divorcee this sadly puts me in the category of 'former' hypocrite.

The greatest lesson we can give or teach our children about love, honesty, integrity, character, etc, etc, etc will be in the form of what they see radiating from mommy and daddy. Kids should not hamper your intimacy but rather take it to the next level. Again, as much as we love our offspring, when they leave we are still commanded to become one with our spouse. This directive is not contingent upon having kids or not having them. It is commanded whether our children are in diapers or about to graduate college. You will have no greater witness than the witness you show your children about how God ordained marriages and that nothing (not even them) should come between these amalgamations.

> *"Therefore, what God has joined together*
> *let not man separate"*
> (Mark 10:9)

So, how do we keep the embers burning when our kids innocently yet frequently douse them with water? I know its easier said than done but from the outset our children need to learn their role in the hierarchy of the home and parents have the daunting task of keeping everything balanced and in perspective. It will be challenging but parents should control the tempo in the home, that's the only way to keep the intimacy between you and your spouse alive and healthy. There's a plethora of literature out there from reputable Christian authors who can give much more seasoned advice on parenting, but it's all for naught if we as parents don't implement the contents and remain puppets on a string to our children.

Our PDA's shouldn't gross our kids out. Our job is to express to them by our actions what God intended for intimacy in marriage, perhaps in doing so they will remain chaste until marriage. They must see the value of a Christian marriage at HOME and hope to emulate the love their parents share. Perhaps through our example our sons will respect women and not call them 'female dogs' and treat them as inferior. Husbands, perhaps in loving your wife 'as Christ loves the church' your daughter will have a clear idea of what a man is supposed to be in and outside of the home.

Perhaps if we set the bar high enough at home when she leaves the nest her 'man radar' will be set with greater standards and she won't bring home that inso-lent dude that calls himself a man. Wives, perhaps by respecting your husband your son won't be enticed by the seductress whose only talent is shaking her booty "like a Polaroid picture". Perhaps our sons can learn to unconditionally love her intellect and purity instead of gazing at her like a brainless piece of meat. We want our children to grow up to be ladies and gentlemen and maybe the intimacy they see in us will show them how to become just that. Our call to become one has implica-tions that go far beyond the bedroom and has the auda-cious potential to affect the next generation. My prayer is that we positively affect them for the glory of God.

Making time at any age and any stage:

Levity: A woman is looking at her naked body in a mirror then looks at her husband and says 'I'm fat, wrinkled, and out of shape, you need to pay me a com-pliment to help bolster my morale and self-esteem' the husband thinks about it for a moment and then replies 'well honey your eyesight is near perfect'.

Understandably, it took some time for the flames of intimacy to diminish in your relationship and it will take time to reignite the flames as well. Three things are essential to keep a fire ablaze; some type of fuel, a spark to ignite it, and oxygen to keep it breathing. Therefore, as it pertains to intimacy and keeping it alive once it gets started, you will have to provide fuel for it to continuously consume (your passion, PDA's etc.) and you will have to blow on it from time to time. Consistency is the key to victory here.

Planning a time to be intimate with your spouse is not a bad strategy but remember you want this to be a tantalizing feast not an arduous routine. There will be many times when spontaneity takes the lead and you both just indulge in one another; that's great when it happens and it's a beautiful thing. An unplanned natural encounter is by far the most toxic and oftentimes most preferred method of engagement. Husbands, there will be times when your wife just wants to be taken with authority and ravished until she can barely lift a finger, other times she wants to be coaxed and enticed.

Wives, believe it or not, guys don't always just want to get straight to 'home plate', we can appreciate and readily enjoy 'all the bases' your glamorous body has to offer. If your husband is lacking in area that you want explored then find a kind way to tell him about it and show him what works for you. Be patient with him when you do this and show that you appreciate his willingness to please you in a way you want to be pleased. Keeping mutuality in mind, find out if there is something he would like differently and submit to his indulgences as well.

Neither of you should be forceful nor demanding if the other is not comfortable with the request, that would be a sin. Let the purity of your love guide your actions in the bedroom and be respectful of each other's boundaries; in time you will both be on equal ground in finding ways to make each other's sex clock tick, and when you do it will be like Big Ben sounding off in your bedroom, you will know exactly what time it is! But who has the time huh? To say we live in a busy world would be a severe understatement. These are the busiest days and times in the history of histories. We have never had so much to do, so many places to go, so much to see, and so much information just a click or two away. There seems to be barely a moment to relax and enjoy the simple things in life. We are inundated with the 'cares of this world' to the point that we forget the ones that should matter to us the most.

I'm just as guilty as the next guy who comes home after a hard days labor or gets home after a church function and greets his sweetheart with a halfhearted hello, a lukewarm kiss on the cheek, grabs a quick bite to eat then plops down on the sofa to watch the ESPN highlights and then fall asleep within fifteen minutes of hyped sound bites. Over time, this becomes routine, the norm of sorts, until one day without even realizing it the fire that once burned so furiously between the sheets is totally and completely distinguished. Frigidity has entered the most holy place in your home and we have sadly become accustomed to its icy presence. What can we do to change this destructive routine? How do we literally break or destroy the ice?

We have to be deliberate in our efforts and make a conscious decision to make time for our mates. Got a day planner, a Blackberry, iPhone, Outlook calendar or any other planning or scheduling assistant? Then set a reasonable timetable to romance your spouse. If you have difficulties being spontaneous then go ahead and make an appointment with the bedroom and then commit to your appointment! Planning to be intimate should not be a chore or a bore, you must use the personality God gave you and let creativity take its course so long as you can both agree on the pleasure principles.

Men, when your wife wants it (your intimate attention) she really, really wants it and you had better be the one to give t to her. If an unbeliever approached you and said 'I'm ready to give my life to Christ what should

I do? Would you turn them away and tell them to come back when it was convenient for you? Would you say you had a headache? I doubt it. So, if you wouldn't make a sinner wait then why would you make a saint?

"Therefore, as we have opportunity, let us do good to all, especially to those who are of the household of faith."
(Galatians 6:10)

A failure to please her innermost sensual needs and desires can be emotionally and spiritually catastrophic and may also be a sin. You don't want to make that mistake. Make time to mate; it's our mandate, our honor, our duty. Put your sermons on pause if you have to and spend a few days and nights basking in the paradise that is your spouse. Study one another in ways you never have before. Brother, ravish your wife with purpose as if it were your wedding night all over again. Sister, get the dust off that lingerie and break out those exotic oils like it's nobody's business. Unfortunately, many of you have let the fire die and are wondering if it's even worth the effort to try and get it burning again. Kids or not, I urge you to take the time to find out, take the time to pray about it sincerely and ask God to direct you in reinvigorating the intimacy between you and your spouse.

He will help you with a plan that works for both of you; a plan that fits you and your growing family; a plan that you are capable of carrying out to fulfillment. Again, we are all in different stages (and ages) of our sensuality so you have to communicate and do what works for you as a couple. Until then, repent for allowing yourself to be so busy that you neglected the flames of intimacy and re-consecrate yourself to doing it right this time around. She will feel loved and elated and he will feel respected like a man again.

Couple Discussion:
- List some of the things you think steal your time away from your spouse and share it with them.
- Would you be willing to talk to or educate your children on the importance of husband & wife quality time?
- What do you think your children are learning about marriage from you?
- Do you make your spouse feel special, loved and respected around your family members, especially your children?

- What are some ways you can do a better job of 'making time'?

- Would you be willing to ask your children, if they are of age, what they see and think of the love mommy and daddy share?

- Would you say that your marriage is an example for other marriages to emulate? If so then how, if not then why?

<u>Prayer:</u>

Dear Lord, we first and foremost want to thank you for the awesome joy and responsibility of a loving family. Thank you for your continued provisions and for never forsaking us in any way. We thank you for the love of our children and ask you to help us to be better parents and role models to the ones you placed in our care. Show us how to let our intimacy reflect a godly love to those we come in contact with and keep us on guard for the enemies attempts to steal precious moments away from us. Give us an open mind and heart to receive new instruction on how to resolve conflicts swiftly and how to be restored stronger and more determined than ever. This we ask in Jesus name, amen.

Chapter 10

The pleasure principles (Size does Matter)

". . .although the challenge with sex in long term relationships is to avoid complacency and boredom, the core of trust often allows people to build on their fantasies and expand the sexual relationship."

(J. Berman & L. Berman, 2001)

*D*oes size really matter as it pertains to our subject of discussion? You bet it does! But not the kind of size you might be thinking of. In this case the size of your efforts is what's going to pay dividends the reinvigoration of your intimacy. So, how big is it? The size of your prayers, are they big? The size of your encouragement, is it big? And the size of your affection, how big is it? Are you honestly doing all you can do to keep the embers burning and maintain the 'attraction' advantage? We all need to gauge this 'self-assessment' of sorts periodically and it is also important to be generous and genuine in the delivery of our 'love' portions.

Being married in Christ, our sensual expression and engagement is without repentance because the creatures' conscience is clear before the creator. Not so for the un-wed unbeliever. . ."fornicators and adulterers God will judge". So what makes your spouse tick sensually? Be advised that knowing what turns them off is equally as important as knowing what turns them on.

Levity: A wife gets naked & asks her hubby, 'What turns you on more, my pretty face or my sexy body?' Hubby looks her up & down and replies, 'Your sense of humor!' (Not so wise huh?)

The Kiss: It is said by some that kissing plays a major role on the stage of intimacy. If this is true then what's the enchantment behind kissing that gives it such potent appeal and influence? I vividly remember my first real kiss. Her name was Laurel, I was nine years old and she was eleven and slightly taller than I. We were playing at a friend's house when she cornered me in a secluded hallway and pulled me close to her and leaned in. It felt like I was being shocked by lightning, I was electrified yet unharmed and whatever strength I had was immediately dispensed. Laurel would be considered one of those 'fast girls' from around the way and at the tender age of ten, she would be instrumental in introducing me to the wonderful world of sex. Think of your first real kiss, do you remember how the butterflies felt in your stomach and how it seemed as if you were floating in the air?

I often wondered if this euphoria could be captured with consistency and at what point does the euphoria fade. I believe the initial anticipation of kissing the one you love has a lot to do with it. Typically at a wedding once vows have been exchanged the presiding official will say to the husband 'you may now kiss the bride'. Why did the husband have to get permission in the first place? Well, back in the day this was the first time an engaged coupe was allowed to kiss and the man was to take the lead in 'breaking the ice'. I know that's not this case in this day and age but in some cultures this is still custom. The kiss is the first step in physical intimacy; it's the key to a door that once opened detonates our hormones into explosive, uncontrollable splendor and eroticism. Holding hands is nice, hugging feels great, but a good kiss is priceless!

Some of you reading this haven't kissed (or been kissed) your spouse in a long time. What gives? Has it lost its allure after so many years or has those once comforting lips turned out to be a dreaded symbol of antagonism and cynicism? You probably feel that the magic is all gone but not so my friend, God cares about your kiss. If you are both still able and willing then there is hope. Remember the anointing we discussed earlier? It is still relevant throughout the reading and application of this book. The anointing will provide you with the 'stuff' you need to put the kick back in your pucker. For starters, you both need to be honest enough to admit that your kissing can use a revival and then you will need to apologize to each other for allowing your kiss to become so stale and insensitive. Then make a promise and a conscious effort to start kissing more each day.

" A wealth of studies now indicate that men and women who enjoy close, supportive, and satisfying

relationships are less physically reactive to external sources of stress, recover more rapidly from illness and have fewer recurrences of serious health problems. . .these are just some of the benefits of a loving and mutually satisfying long term relationship"
(S. Wolf, 2007)

As you enjoy the comeback, solicit mutual input from your spouse, be patient, sincere and have fun. Whether you decide to have an open or closed mouth kiss is irrelevant, the idea is to make it real and full of emotion. There are times of course when a long kiss isn't practical and only a quick peck will suffice; no problem. Just make sure that try to make up for it at your earliest convenience. From now on be determined to put the old ways of meaningless kissing behind you and look forward with excitement to a fantastic future of stimulating smooching. Finally, your kiss is your signature or calling card to your spouse that says 'I'm still attracted to you and I still desire you'. These statements speak volumes as you are both bombarded with worldly interruptions and distractions.

Another caveat to consider is the size and content of what you say to your spouse. Even what you don't say can be equally deafening, body language is still communication so be careful. Let's take the time to be complementary to our spouses, fill their ears with accolades and encouragement. Each time you see each other should be like going to the gas station to fill up your tank. Fill one another with words that bless and heal; this is something that can be encouraging and habit forming. I enjoy watching my wife go about her daily routines; she often catches my gaze and I smile ever so slightly letting her know that I am indeed admiring and lusting after her. She loves it!

We have both formed the habit of speaking praise on each other and there's no other place we would rather be that in the comfort of each other's arms. We share the peace in knowing that our words are carefully chosen and that we can find solace, rest and erotica in our communication.

Making love or having sex? Is there really a difference between making love and having sex? Well, we generally tend to think of sex as an animalistic act filled with abrupt sequences of erotica while 'love making' is seen as a more deliberate and passionate activity. Regardless of the interpretation, for the born again believer every phase of intimacy (hugging, kissing, caressing, intercourse. . .) fall under the category of making love. Making love to your spouse starts long before you actually have intercourse. Every PDA, every thought, every look, every flirt, kiss, and every embrace is love in the making! And yes, size does matter ☺

Conclusion

—⚶—

"**F**inally my brethren. . .think on these things". Much has been covered in these ten short chapters, where you go from here is entirely up to you. As for me and my house, by the grace of God we will continue to pursue prosperity in our ever evolving intimacy. Thank you for taking the time to review these pages; it's my continued prayer that the affection in your relationship will be restored and strengthened for the journey ahead. I do hope that you realize how precious, fragile and fleeting our time with each other is; and I pray that we purposely seize each moment as a cherished opportunity to bring God glory in our unions. I'm so very excited about the feedback we have received thus far and for the many couples who have rededicated themselves to each other and have decided to take their intimacy back from the enemy.

We know that this will be a constant challenge for us and that we have to be vigilant now more than ever. May God bless and keep us so on that day of accountability we can say with confidence and conviction that in this particular area of ministry that we too have kept the faith and have fought the good fight.

Press on!

Yours in Christ,

Chaz Konani

About the Author

—⚏—

Chaz Konani was born and raised in Brooklyn New York. He served in the United States Marine Corps and began traveling the world at the young age of eighteen. Much of what has been documented in this writing is the result of eyewitness accounts and personal tragedy. It is thru his own failures that Chaz has had the privilege of providing unofficial and unsolicited counsel to several couples thru the years. He now lives in California and is married with three children.

Note to Salvation Seekers

—∿—

*D*ear salvation seeker, God loves you, He always has and He always will. It is my greatest joy, privilege, honor and commission to introduce to you the one and only Savior of the world. His name is Jesus Christ and His story of redeeming mankind is foretold in the Old Testament of the Holy Bible and brought to fruition in the New Testament. I recommend reading the gospels (good news) told in the New Testament books of Mathew, Mark, Luke & John. I would also challenge you to do some critical thinking and research on ANY god or claimed deity and you will find that none will compare to Jesus the Christ. Not one will come even close. Furthermore, none can claim that they were God manifested in flesh so that they could sacrifice them-selves to die as a substitute for sinful man and then to not stay dead but to ultimately defeat death itself; never to die again. He indeed lives and no one but Jesus can boast such a claim as our resurrected Lord and King.

It is thru this Jesus that we Christians live, hope and breathe. All the 'work' of the salvation of man was done thru Jesus Christ, nothing you or I could do can ever replace His finished work. Jesus Christ literally bridged the gap between God and man and has become the only way to our heavenly father. So, in order to be saved we must first believe in Him and who He is. This acknowledgement is a crucial first step of faith that we take in order to walk with Him for the rest of our lives so consider it with the utmost consideration. Secondly, repentance (ask for forgiveness) of our sins, once we acknowledge Christ as Lord of our lives our true conviction will be evident in this next step of asking God to forgive us for our sins against Him and thanking Him for sending His son Jesus to die in our stead. Jesus literally paid a debt that we ourselves could not pay; He stepped in and became sin, destroyed its eternal grip on our souls and rose from the grave in complete and total victory.

Lastly, accept what Jesus Christ has already done on your behalf, welcoming Him into your heart and allowing Him via His Holy spirit to begin a transformation in your life for His majestic glory. Having done this you would now be a 'new creation' in Christ Jesus, old things are passed away and all things are made new. Jesus told us that He would soon return once again to this earth and that He would gather his saints to join Him in heaven and there we will forever be with our Lord. That time is at hand my friend, I do hope and pray you decide to join us.

If you have further inquiries please send us an email at chaz.konani@gmail.com or visit your local bible based church where truth is taught and you can grow in your faith and newfound walk in Christ.

That's salvation 101 my friend, I highly recommend that you take the time to seek out the Savior while He may yet be found.

In Christ,
Chaz

Appendix A

Couple Interview Questions

—◊—

1. How long have you been married?

2. How many times have you been married?

3. Do you have children? If yes how many?

4. Do you pray about your sex life or lack of a sex life? How often?

5. What is your definition of an attractive (or sexy) man/woman?

6. If you have erotic fantasies do you share them with your spouse? Why or why not?

7. Do you consider yourself and your spouse sexy or attractive? How so?

8. Does your spouse make you feel desired, wanted or sexy? How so?

9. Fill in the blanks and feel free to elaborate: As it pertains to our intimacy if my spouse would _____ then I would _____.

10. What do YOU consider sensually satisfying or how would you define a 'healthy' sex life?

11. Do you and your spouse still 'date' each other? How so?

12. What was the most exciting sensual time you've had with your spouse and what do you think changed it for better or worse?

13. Does your spouse currently excite you and consider your sensual pleasure? Please explain or give an example.

14. Do you intentionally set aside 'quality' time for each other? How so?

15. Are orgasms common for you with your spouse? If no, why not?

16. Have you or your spouse done something in your relationship that has caused a seemingly incurable scar or damper to your intimacy?

17. If you could gauge intimacy on a thermometer what would the average temperature be in your home?

18. What areas of intimacy would you like to see your spouse improve? How can he/she satisfy your needs more?

19. What areas of your intimacy could you improve upon? How can you be more pleasing or appealing?

20. Finish this sentence: I feel most intimate when my spouse. . .?

21. What causes you to lose interest in being intimate with your spouse?

22. If you could go back to a specifically joyful and sensual time in your relationship, when would that be?

23. How often do you pray for strength and the willingness to be more intimate with your spouse?

24. Have you ever worked through infidelity in your relationship or suspected infidelity in your relationship? How so?

25. Do you feel that there is a 'stranger' in your bedroom perhaps occupying the mind of your spouse?

26. Do you share PDA's (Public displays of affection) or not? Explain.

27. Aside from intercourse, what turns you on about your significant other?

28. Do you agree that the Church should take the lead on such a 'taboo' topic? Why or why not?

29. How can the church be more helpful in putting sensual intimacy into perspective and taking it back from a perverted world without being perverted?

30. If there were undefiled intimacy classes in your local church would you attend and participate?

References/Bibliography

1. Berman, J. & Berman L., (2001) For Women Only, *a revolutionary guide to overcoming sexual dysfunction and reclaiming your sex life.* New York: Henry Holt and Company, LLC.
2. Bridges, J., (2006) The Discipline of Grace. Colorado Springs, CO: NavPress.
3. Emerson, E., (2004) Love & Respect. Nashville, TN: Thomas Nelson, Inc.
4. Pope T. P., (2010) For Better, *the science of a good marriage.* New York: The Penguin Group Inc.
5. Heller, K. (2012). The Myth of the High Rate of Divorce. Psych Central. Retrieved on February 14, 2013, from http://psychcentral.com/lib/2012/the-myth-of-the-high-rate-of-divorce/

6. "Divorce Custom: 7 Post-Split Rituals from around the World." HuffPost. July 21, 2012. Accessed: October 12, 2012.

7. "Divorce Statistics." Divorce Statistics. 2012. Accessed: October 13, 2012.

8. "Divorce Stats in the U.S. by Age and Region of the Country." Family Law Courts. 2010-2012. Accessed: October 13, 2012.

9. Hardy, Marcelina. "Top Reasons for Divorce." Love to Know.10.

10. Wolf. S., (2007) This Old Spouse, *a do-it-yourself guide to restoring, renovating, and rebuilding your relationship.* New York: The Penguin Group, Inc.

11. http://facts.randomhistory.com/divorce-facts.html

CPSIA information can be obtained at www.ICGtesting.com
Printed in the USA
BVOW032056230413

318937BV00002B/254/P